PONIES PAST AND PRESENT

PONIES PAST AND PRESENT

WALTER GILBEY

Zone Press

CONTENTS

The increasing attention which during the last few years has been devoted to
breeding ponies for various purposes, more especially for polo, suggested the
collection of facts relating to our half-wild races of ponies. It will be seen from
the following pages that we possess large supplies of small but strong and sound
constitutional horses which may be turned to far more valuable account than
has been done hitherto. The Polo Pony Society set the example of drawing attention to the possibilities of utilizing profitably the Moorland and Forest Mares,
and it is hoped that these pages may be of some interest to those who are giving
attention to pony breeding whether for polo or for any other purpose.

Elsenham Hall, Essex, August 1900

To Exclu$ive

You were the best pony ever.

Publisher's Note

For the Updated Edition of Ponies: Past and Present. Originally Published in 1900 by Sir Walter Gilbey

When *Ponies: Past and Present* first appeared in 1900, it was written with the confidence of a man who believed in categories: in breeds and bloodlines, in historical order, in the value of looking backward to understand what lies ahead. Sir Walter Gilbey, a baronet and wine merchant with a passion for horses, brought together his observations on native British ponies—not just as animals, but as quiet partners in the building of a country.

This book, a companion of sorts to Gilbey's earlier and work *Horses: Past and Present*, focuses on ponies: their shapes and temperaments, their regional origins, and their steady usefulness in the lives of people.

It was written at a time when ponies still worked for their living, pulling carts, carrying loads, and helping in the fields.

A great deal has changed since then. Ponies are no longer tools of labor, at least not in most parts of the world. They've become athletes, companions, show animals, therapy animals, even internet stars. And yet, much remains the same: ponies are still sturdy, intelligent, a little stubborn, and often deeply loved.

This edition keeps the original text mostly as Gilbey wrote it.

We have updated some of the spelling and grammar for the modern reader, while keeping some of the original writings, quotations from documents, and images to maintain Gilbey's voice and mood.

The editor has also taken the liberty of imagining what Gilbey might think about ponies in the 21st century—how he might respond to the way they live now, and how their legacy continues. These additions are not meant to rewrite Gilbey's perspective, but to bring it gently forward in time.

We hope this new edition helps readers—especially younger ones—see ponies not just as part of the past, but as living creatures with a fascinating history that stretches into today. Gilbey wrote about ponies with care and conviction. This edition tries to do the same.

—The Editor
September 2025

A word about ponies from the year 1900

Over the last century, growing interest in breeding ponies for a wide range of uses—especially polo—has brought renewed attention to Britain's semi-wild native pony breeds. This work brings together key facts about this hardy, often overlooked animals. As the following pages show, the British Isles are home to a substantial number of small, tough, and resilient ponies which, until the 20th century, remained largely underutilized—despite their clear potential for valuable and practical work.

The Polo Pony Society plays a significant role in this story, being among the first to recognize the potential of Moorland and Forest Mares. Their early advocacy sets an important example of how native breeds can be developed and turned to profitable and sustainable use. This material is offered in the hope that it will be of real interest to anyone engaged in pony breeding—whether for polo, riding, driving, or broader equestrian pursuits.

Today, in the 21st century, the descendants of these native ponies continue to prove their worth far beyond the polo field. Their long-standing reputation for hardiness and sure-footedness remains, but thanks to selective breeding and thoughtful training, many have emerged as top performers in modern equestrian sports. In hunter-jumper arenas in particular, ponies are celebrated for their agility, balance, and intelligent temperaments—traits that make them ideal mounts for both young riders and adults. From local shows to international competition, these once-overlooked breeds are now recognized not as rural curiosities, but as capable and versatile athletes in their own right.

Among Britain's best native pony breeds, several bloodlines have gained particular distinction in recent years. The Connemara pony continues to lead in international recognition, with stallions such as *Gwen-*

nic de Goariva and *I Love You Melody* producing top-tier offspring for show jumping and eventing.

The Welsh pony, especially from Section B lines, also enjoys a strong reputation in hunter-jumper and sport pony breeding programs. Influential sires like *Sleight of Hand, Downland Chevalier, Cusop Dimension,* and *Eyarth Rio* have shaped generations of athletic, elegant ponies admired for their movement, temperament, and type.

Meanwhile, the Dartmoor pony, though traditionally associated with children's mounts, has seen a resurgence, with sires such as *Shilstone Rocks North Westerly* contributing to breeding programs that prioritize quality, conformation, and a willing disposition. Together, these native breeds—and the bloodlines that sustain them—demonstrate that Britain's ponies are not merely part of equestrian history, but essential players in its present and future.

• WG 1900 & 2025

Painted by A. Cooper, R.A.   Engraved on wood by F. Babbage.

THE SHOOTING PONY.

CHAPTER 1

Introduction

In my other volume, *Horses Past and Present*, brief reference has been made to the early subjugation of the horse in Eastern countries by man; and it is unnecessary here to further touch upon that phase of our subject.

The early history of the horse in the British Islands is obscure. The animal is not indigenous to the country, and it is supposed that the original stock was brought to England many centuries before the Christian era by the Phoenician navigators who visited the shores of Cornwall to procure supplies of tin.

However that may be, the first historian who rendered any account of our islands for posterity found horses here which he regarded as of exceptional merit. Julius Caesar, when he invaded Britain in the year 55 B.C., was greatly impressed with the strength, handiness, and docility of the horses which the ancient Britons drove in their war chariots. His laudatory description of their merits includes no special remarks concerning their size, and from this omission we may infer that they were not much larger than the breeds of horses with which Caesar's travels and conquests had already made him acquainted.

There can be no doubt but that these historical chariot horses were small by comparison with their descendants—the modern Shire horses. They probably did not often exceed 14 hands, and were therefore much on a par in point of height with the horses Caesar had seen in Spain and elsewhere.

It is unlikely that so shrewd an observer would have refrained from comment on the point of size had the British horses been greatly inferior or superior in size, as they were in qualities, to the breeds he already knew.

It is doubtful indeed whether the horses of Britain gained in stature to any material extent until the Saxons and Danes introduced horses from the Continent. These, being for military purposes, would certainly have been stallions without exception, and being larger than the British breed, must have done something to produce an increase of height when crossed with our native mares.

This being the case, we are confronted with the difficulty of distinguishing between the horses and ponies of these early times.

Most chroniclers do not attempt to differentiate between "horse" and "pony" as we now understand the terms. The process of developing a big horse was necessarily a slow one, from the system, or rather the want of system, which remained in vogue until the fifteenth century, and was still in existence in some parts of England in Henry VIII's time (that is to say, from June 28, 1491, through January 28, 1547).

During this long period, the greater portion of the country lay under forest and waste, and it was the practice to let those mares which were kept solely for breeding purposes run at large in the woodlands, unbroken and unhandled.

We learn this in part from The Doomsday Book, an 11th-century manuscript that records a highly detailed survey of England and parts of Wales; the book was commissioned by King William the Conqueror in 1086 to understand his new kingdom's resources for administrative and taxation purposes. It contains extensive information on land holdings, resources like mills and vineyards, and population, providing a unique snapshot of pre-industrial society that remains a vital historical resource.

The book contains frequent mention of *equæ silvestres, equæ silvaticæ,* or *equæ indomitæ* when enumerating the livestock on a manor; and there is evidence to show that these animals (always mares, it will be observed) were under a modified degree of supervision.

The mares were branded to prove their ownership, and during the summertime, selected mares appear to have been "rounded up" to an enclosure in the forest for service. Apart from this, they largely ranged the country at large, strangers alike to collar and bridle.

It would be unreasonable to suppose that the mares which were employed in agricultural work were not also used for breeding; the surroundings for the farmer's mare in those days were not luxurious, but she undoubtedly enjoyed shelter from the rigors of winter and more nourishing food than her woodland sister. Hence it is probable that the first differences in size, make, and shape among English horses may be traced to the treatment of their domestic or woodland ancestry on the dam's side.

The life led by these *equae indomitae* made for a certain hardiness of constitution, soundness of limb, surefootedness, and small stature. And we venture to think that the half-wild ponies England possesses today in the New Forest, Exmoor, Wales, and the Fell country are (or were, until comparatively modern efforts were made to improve them) the lineal descendants of the woodland stock which is frequently referred to in ancient records, and which in 1535 and 1541 Henry VIII made, as you shall learn, vigorous attempts to exterminate.

Shocking as it may sound today, the law of 1535 (26 Henry VIII) declares:—

"For that in many and most places of this realm, commonly little horses and nags of small stature and value be suffered to departure, and also to cover mares and fillies of very small stature, by reason whereof the breed of good and strong horses of this realm is now lately diminished, altered and decayed, and further is likely to decay if speedy remedy be not sooner provided in that behalf.

It is provided that all owners or farmers of parks and enclosed grounds of the extent of one mile in compass shall keep two mares, apt and able to bear foals of the altitude or height of 13 handfuls at least, upon pain of 40s.

A penalty of 40s. is imposed on the Lords, Owners, and Farmers of all parks and grounds enclosed, as is above rehearsed, who shall willingly suffer any of the said mares to be covered or kept with any Stoned Horse under the stature of 14 handfuls."

Essentially, this law, and the fines associated with breaking it, 40 shillings (which was a rather substantial sum at the time) was trying to stop the breeding of small, weak horses by requiring landowners to maintain larger mares and prevent small stallions from being used for breeding.

This Act applied only to enclosed areas, and therefore would not affect the wild ponies in any appreciable degree: but six years later another Act was passed (32 Henry VIII, c. 13) which provided that—

"No person shall put in any forest, chase, moor, heath, common, or waste (where mares and fillies are used to be kept) any stoned horse above the age of two years, not being fifteen hands high within the Shires and territories of Norfolk, Suffolk, Cambridge, Buckingham, Huntingdon, Essex, Kent, South Hampshire, North Wiltshire, Oxford, Berkshire, Worcester, Gloucester, Somerset, South Wales, Bedford, Warwick, Northampton, Yorkshire, Cheshire, Staffordshire, Lancashire, Salop, Leicester, Hereford and Lincoln.

And furthermore, be it enacted, that if in any of the said drifts there shall be found any mare, filly, foal, or gelding that then shall be thought not to be able nor like to grow to be able to bear foals of reasonable stature or not able nor like to grow to be able to do profitable labors by the discretions of the drivers aforesaid or of the more number of them, then the same driver or drivers shall cause the same unprofitable beasts ... every of them to be killed, and the bodies of them to be buried in the ground, as no annoyance thereby shall come or grow to the people, those near inhabiting or thither resorting."

Essentially, this law required that only large, strong horses be kept for breeding, and any undersized or unfit animals found on common lands were to be destroyed to improve the overall quality of horse stock. This enactment was of a more far-reaching character than its forerunner. The "shires and territories" enumerated were those in which greatest attention was paid to the breeding of Great Horses.

"Profitable labors," in those times, could only mean military service, agricultural work, and perhaps pack transport, for any of which purposes the woodland ponies were useless. How far the law proved effectual is another matter: laws more nearly affecting the welfare of the subject were less honored in the observance than the breach in the remoter parts of the kingdom in those times.

In 1566, when Elizabeth was on the throne, Thomas Blundeville, of Newton Flotman, wrote a book on *Horses and Riding*; and prefaced it by a formal "Epistle dedicatorie" to Robert Lord Dudley, Master of the Horse, which begins:

> "It would be the means that the Queen may not only cause such statutes touching the breeding of Horses upon Commons to be put in execution: but also that all such parks within the Realm as be in Her Highnesses hands and meet for that purpose might not wholly be employed to the keeping of Deer (which is altogether without profit), but partly to the necessary breeding of Horses for service [*i.e.*, military service] whereof this Realm of all others at this instant hath greatest need."

Here, Blundeville urges the Queen to repurpose some royal deer parks into horse-breeding grounds to strengthen England's supply of war horses.

So, it would appear that Henry's laws had become a dead letter, or something very like it, within twenty-five years of its finding place on the Statute Book. It was afterwards repealed in respect of certain counties by Queen Elizabeth and James I. (for particulars on these matters see p. 26 and p. 33 in my *"Horses Past and Present."*)

These various early edicts no doubt produced some result in the more central parts of England, though, as we gather from Blundeville's "Epistle," those charged with their administration failed to enforce them in areas more remote.

A certain amount of driving and killing no doubt was done, but probably no more than enough to make the herds wilder than before and send them in search of safety to the most inaccessible districts.

The natural result of this would have been to preserve the breeds in greater purity than would have been the case had they been allowed to intermingle with horses which, after the harvest was carried, were turned out to graze at will over the unfenced fields and commons.

It is worth glancing at these items of horse legislation to discover that the half-wild ponies and their legacy have survived, not by grace of man's aid or protection, but rather in defiance of his endeavors to stamp them out!

Nearly a century later (1658), the Duke of Newcastle published his work on the *Feeding, Dressing and Training of Horses for the Great Saddle* and therein, urged strongly the desirability of discouraging the breeding of ponies. The records of subsequent reigns show occasional efforts to improve by legislation the breeds of horses needed for military purposes, tournaments, racing and sport, but until we come to the time of George II, we find no *positive* attempt to discourage the breeding of ponies.

An Act passed in 1740 was definite enough in the purpose it sought to attain. This was the suppression of races by "poneys" and other small or weak horses.

Under this law, matches for prizes under £50 were forbidden, save at Newmarket and Black Hambleton, and the weights to be carried by horses were fixed at 10 stone for a five-year-old (140 pounds), 11 stone. (154 pounds) for a six-year-old and 12 stone (168 pounds) for a seven-year-old horse. This statute had two-fold intention: it was framed "not only to prevent the encouragement of a vile and paltry breed of horses, but also to remove all temptation from the lower class of people who constantly attend these races, to the great loss of time and hindrance of labor, and whose behavior still calls for stricter regulations to curb their licentiousness and correct their manners."

But during the 20th century, organized efforts to improve these breeds has followed recognition of their possibilities for usefulness, and in few localities, if any, does the original stock remain pure. In Devonshire, Hampshire, Wales, Cumberland, the Highlands, Shetland, and in the West of Ireland, the original strains have been intermingled and alien blood introduced.

Small Thoroughbred, Arabians and Hackney sires have produced new and improved breeds less fitted to withstand the rigors of winter and the effects of scanty food contingent on independent and useless existence, but infinitely better calculated to serve the interests of mankind.

Before the establishment of the Hackney Horse Society in 1883, the dividing line between the horse and the pony in England was vague and undefined. It was then found necessary to distinguish clearly between horses and ponies, and accordingly all animals measuring 14 hands or under were designated "ponies," and registered in a separate part of the Stud Book.

This record of height, with other particulars as to breeding, serves to direct breeders in their choice of sires and dams. The standard of height established by the Hackney Horse Society was accepted and officially recognized by the Royal Agricultural Society in 1889, when the prize list for the Windsor Show contained pony classes for animals not exceeding 14 hands.

The altered Polo-rule which fixes the limit of height at 14 hands 2 inches may be productive of some little confusion; but for all other purposes 14 hands is the recognized maximum height of a pony. Prior to 1883 small horses were called by many different names: galloways, hobbies, cobs, or ponies, irrespective of their height. A pony in 2025 is generally under 14.2 hands at the wither.

The opening of the First Seal: St John, and the Rider on the White Horse
represented as Christ with a sword (early 14th century).

CHAPTER 2

The New Forest Pony

The New Forest in Hampshire now cover some 63,000 acres of which about 42,000 acres are common pasture, the remaining 21,000 acres having been enclosed in 1851 for the growth of timber.

The greater portion of the common land is poor and boggy moor, and on these areas, ponies have been bred in a semi-wild state from the earliest of times. It is considered more than probable that the New Forest ponies are the survival of the stock which, before the time of Canute (1017-1035), was found in the district formerly called Ytene, and which was afforested in the year 1072 by the Conqueror.

On the 15th of March 1217, Henry III (1216-1272), ordered the Warden of the pony stud kept in the New Forest to give to the Monks of Beaulieu all the profits accruing from the droves from that date until November 1220. This donation was for the benefit of the soul of his late father, King John. So, we can see that the New Forest ponies of the thirteenth century were numerous enough to form a source of revenue to the Crown.

The remote history of the breed need not concern us; for it was not until comparatively recent times that any endeavor was made towards the improvement of the "forester," as it is called.

The first infusion of alien blood likely to be beneficial seems to have been made in about 1766; and the circumstances under which this fresh blood was introduced are very interesting.

In 1750, H.R.H. the Duke of Cumberland acquired by exchange a thoroughbred foal from his breeder, Mr. John Hutton. The animal was named Marske and was raced at Newmarket. Achieving no great success on the turf, he was put to the stud, but up until the time of the Duke's death, his progeny had done nothing special to win reputation for their sire.

When the Duke died, in 1765, his horses were sold at Tattersall's, and Marske was knocked down "for a song" to a Dorsetshire farmer. The farmer kept him in the New Forest district, and here Marske, the sire of Eclipse, served mares at a fee of half-a-guinea, till his famous son achieved celebrity.

Eclipse was foaled in 1764, won his first race on April 3' 1769, at Epsom. Eclipse made his big name in a single season on the turf.

For four years at least, therefore (until Mr. Wildman ferreted out "the sire of Eclipse" and bought him for £20 to go to Yorkshire), the New Forest breed of ponies was being improved by an infusion of the very best thoroughbred blood, the effects of which continued to be apparent for many years after Marske had left the district.

It is at least probable that Marske ran in the Forest during the lifetime of the Duke of Cumberland; for that prince was Warden of the New Forest, and the evidence shows that the Duke made a systematic attempt to better the stamp of pony.

For many decades after this infusion of thoroughbred blood, nothing was done to maintain the improvement. On the contrary, the demand for New Forest ponies increased, and the commoners took advantage of the higher prices obtainable to sell the best of their young stock. And this is why the breed steadily degenerated, until the late Prince Consort sent a grey Arabian stallion to stand at New Park.

The effects of this fresh strain of blood were soon evident; but history, as exemplified by the beneficial results of Marske's service, repeated itself; the commoners were all too ready to sell the pick of the young animals, whereby the benefits which should have accrued were heavily discounted.

It must be explained that the large breeders have running in the Forest a hundred ponies, or even more; many breeders possess forty or fifty, while the small occupiers own as many as they can keep during the winter. Their sole responsibility to the Crown in respect of the ponies is the "marking fee" (raised in 1897 from eighteen pence to two shillings per head), which goes to the Verderer's Court. The marking system enables the Court to know how many ponies are running in the Forest, and the latest census showed about 3,000 animals, of which it was estimated some 1,800 were breeding mares.

From spring to autumn, the droves ranged the Forest at will, affecting, of course, the best pasturage, or, in the heat of summer, the shadiest localities; in winter about 1800 ponies are taken into pastures, with the remaining 1200 being left to roam at large.

It is to be observed that the most profitable animals are the hardy ones, which run in the Forest all the year round. The majority of the young animals are handled only for the purpose of marking, and are never, if possible, driven off their own ground. Thus, unless strange stallions are used, it is very difficult to change the blood, the forest-born stallion remaining in his own locality and collecting his own harem around him.

"In-and-in" breeding is therefore inevitable. Besides these 3,000 ponies, it is estimated that about the Forest neighborhood some 2,000 ponies are worked in light carts and other vehicles, and, as many of these ponies are used for breeding purposes, it will be seen what an important source of pony supply we have in the New Forest district.

When the influence of the Arab sire sent by the Prince Consort ceased to be felt, degeneration again set in, the decreased prices brought by ponies at the fairs proving conclusively how the breed was deteriorating.

To combat the evil, the Court of Verderers in 1885 hired four well-bred stallions, which were kept by the "Agisters," or markers of ponies, for the service of commoners' mares at nominal fees.

Two seasons' experience proved that funds would not bear the strain, and the horses were sold; with the less hesitation because it was found that in the absence of any inducement to the breeders to retain promising young stock, good foals and bad were alike sent for sale to the fairs.

Moreover, the wild mares were not of course covered by these stallions, and the majority of the New Forest stock obtained no benefit from their presence in the district.

The "ponies in hand," nevertheless, were more than sufficiently numerous to be considered, and in 1889 it was arranged to provide the necessary inducement to keep promising youngsters by giving premiums at a stallion show in April of each year, winners of premiums to run in the Forest till the following August. This scheme has been productive of very marked results in the way of keeping good stock to reproduce their kind.

Her Majesty in 1889 lent two Arab stallions, Abeyan and Yirassan, for use in the district, and these, remaining for two and three seasons respectively, did a great deal of good. A son of the former, out of a Welsh mare, now stands in the district. His owner, a Mr. Moens, states that his produce show great improvement, and his services are in eager demand among the commoners. The general improvement in the Forest ponies since 1890 is very striking.

Lack of funds has seriously handicapped the New Forest Pony Association in its work, and the burden of carrying out the program has fallen upon the shoulders of a few. Conspicuous among those who have borne the lion's share of the task is Lord Arthur Cecil, who now turns out no fewer than twenty-two stallions for the benefit of the commoners generally.

For many years past, Lord Arthur has interested himself in the improvement of the breed; he has been using with much success stallions of a distinct and pure breed from the Island of Rum off the West coast of Scotland.

These are the wonderful original "Black Galloways" which were found in a wild state on the island in 1840 by the late Marquis of Salisbury and were always kept pure. Lord Arthur secured the whole stock in the year 1888.

I cannot do better than give, practically in its entirety, his interesting letter on the subject of these ponies which for the last ten years have been increasingly used in the New Forest so much to the advantage of the breed:

> "The Rum ponies which were much thought of by my father seem to be quite a type of themselves, having characteristics which would almost enable one to recognize them anywhere. Every one of those I bought in 1888 had *hazel*, not *brown* eyes; and though only a small boy in 1862, when six or seven of those ponies came to Hatfield, I can remember that they also had the special hazel eye.
>
> They have, almost without exception, very good hindquarters, with the tail well set up; and it is in this respect that I hope they will do good in the New Forest.
>
> On the other hand, they have big plain heads which are not liked by the commoners. This defect, however, is rapidly disappearing with good keep, as it does with all breeds of ponies.
>
> After I bought the ponies in 1888 and began breeding them, I was at a loss to know how to continue the breed, as I could not well use the stallion which accompanied the mares to his own progeny.
>
> But I remembered having seen at the Highland and Agricultural Society's Show, in 1883, a stallion, Laddie, which had interested me very much, being exactly like the ponies I remembered coming to Hatfield.
>
> I enclose ... copy of a letter received from his breeder:

'The pony, Highland Laddie ... was bred by us at Coul-more, Ross-shire; being the youngest, I think, of seven foals thrown by the black mare, Polly, to Allan Kingsburgh (Lord Lovat's stallion) ... and, as far as I know, Polly was never covered by any other horse.

Most of her foals, if not all, were shown by us and won prizes at country and the Highland Agricultural Society's Meetings in the North.

Her third foal, Glen, a jet-black stallion, took 2nd prize in his class at the Aberdeen Show in 1880 (I think), and again took the medal for pony stallions at Perth in 1881 or 1882. At the same show Polly's second foal, Blackie, took second prize in the gelding class, and her fourth foal (the eldest of the bay mares), shown at Inverness by McKenzie of Kintail, would easily have taken a prize in her class but for an accident on the railway or ferry ... which lamed her for the meeting.

Your pony has, of course, the same pedigree as those.... The Rum ponies were always supposed to be pure, as the Marquis of Salisbury was known to take a great interest in the breed ... though I am not sure, I believe a pony stallion of another strain, a dun with black mane and tail (Lord Ronald) was sold by my father to go to Rum.... Allan Kingsburgh and Polly were both bred by my father.... Allan's dam was a bay mare, Polly's was a grey named Maria.

I know the stock from which both came: it was brought long ago from Glenelg and bred and kept pure by my grandfather and ancestors who lived in Glenelg when that Barony belonged to the MacLeod of MacLeods. I am not sure of the sires of either Allan or Polly, but know they were both pure Highland. One, I think, was Lord Ronald which I formerly mentioned, and the other a pony belonging to a Mr. Stewart in Skye (a known breeder of Highland cattle).

... It is curious that I should have thus dropped on to exactly the same kind of thing that my father is supposed to have used; he used the same blood years ago in Lord Ronald.

I think what first interested me so much in these ponies was that, as long ago as I can remember anything, I heard my father describing them to old Lord Cowley and the Duke of Wellington.

He told them how like the Spanish horses he had thought the ponies in 1845; and mentioned how he had turned down a stallion on the island and a Spanish jack-ass—some of the mules are still at Hatfield. And that was in 1889. He also said that he saw no reason why they should not be descended from some of the Spanish Armada horses which were wrecked on that coast.

When the ponies—most of them stallions—came to Hatfield in 1862, I remember some of them broke out of the station; it took several days to catch them again. They were almost unbreakable, but my brother, Lionel, and I managed to get two of them sufficiently quiet for *us* to ride, though they would not have been considered safe conveyances for an elderly gentleman.

We were never quite sure of their age, but they must have been nearly thirty when they died.

I believe my father had intended these ponies to be kept entire, but they were so hopelessly savage they had to be cut. They could trot twelve miles in fifty-five minutes after they were twenty years old and could gallop and jump anything in the saddle.

My father's theory about the Spanish Armada receives curious corroboration in the well-known fact that a galleon lies sunk in Tobermory Bay. There was a small map in the "Armada" number of the *Illustrated London News* which was published in 1888 (the same year that I bought the ponies), which showed the storms off the North and West of Scotland, which are almost exactly co-incident with the occurrence of this particular type of pony, though no place was so favorable for breeding a type as a remote island like Rum.

When my mother visited Rum, the people of the adja-cent island of Canna gave her a pony mare which I also re-member, very old, at Hatfield. She was a rich cream color; she threw a foal which had all the characteristics: the hazel eye, long croup, and big head.

I have noticed all the deer-stalking ponies I could see on the look-out for some of these characteristics. But, with the exception of the hazel eye and a somewhat strong incli-nation towards blackness in color, I cannot say that I have noticed much trace of the same kind of pony on the main-land in Scotland.

This, however, is no doubt rather the result of crossing with other strains than because they do not have not some of the original blood. I feel sure that the Galloway of olden days was of the same type, though that term has now come to mean something quite different and in no way con-nected with the district on the West Coast of Scotland.

The hazel eye is not uncommon on Exmoor and occurs in the Welsh pony. It would be a very interesting study to try and trace the tendency to show that color. It would, I think, throw light on the ancestry of many horses and ponies; or, at least, it would reveal many curious instances of *reversion*."

Lord Arthur, in conclusion, deprecates the susceptibility of pony breeders generally to the influence of fashion. He is of opinion that efforts were made in some districts to increase size, while efforts elsewhere are directed to its reduction, which cannot in the long run be beneficial. Whereas, if Nature were allowed to determine the size of pony suitable for each locality, valuable results might be obtained by crossing the different breeds.

It is quite certain that the perpetuation of a breed larger than the character of the country and pasture can support can only be secured by the constant introduction of alien blood, which in the course of time will completely alter the local stamp, and not necessarily for the better.

The Hon. Gerald Lascelles, Deputy Surveyor of the New Forest, has said of this locality: "You have a magnificent run for your ponies. Your mares might breed from ponies of almost any quality.... Ponies running out all winter in the mountains of Ireland and of Wales, on Exmoor, in Cornwall, and on the Cumberland and Yorkshire fells, have a far worse climate to face than that of the New Forest, and no better pasture. Such ponies would laugh at the hardships of the New Forest."

The New Forest pony is perhaps less hardy than some of the hill breeds, but his constitution is quite robust enough to be one of his most valuable attributes; and opinions are not unnaturally divided as to the desirability of increasing his size, if gain of inches mean sacrifice of hardiness. Thirteen hands was the height the Forest breeders formerly admitted to be the maximum desirable; but of recent years their views on this point have been somewhat enlarged.

The close resemblance of the Rum ponies to the native of the New Forest marks out these stallions as peculiarly suitable for crossing purposes. For this reason, and also because their number must exercise strong and speedy influence upon the wild Forest mares, the foregoing particulars have been given in detail.

Lord Arthur believes that the Welsh pony stallion of about 13.1 or 13.2 would be as good a cross for the New Forest pony as any now obtainable.

Lord Ebrington, who bought Exmoor and the Simonsbath stud of improved Exmoor ponies, lent one of his stallions to the New Forest Association in the summer of 1898, and this sire has done good service among the wild mares.

When broke, the New Forest ponies are generally far more spirited than the ordinary run of British ponies. The practice of using the "ponies in hand" for driving the wild mobs to be branded, teaches them to turn quickly and gallop collectedly on rough ground; they thus acquire great cleverness.

As regards their market value, the following letter from Mr. W. J. C. Moens, a most energetic member of the Council of the Association, gives the best idea.

"At the last Ringwood Fair, December 11th, 1897, there was a larger outside demand for suckers than ever experienced; buyers coming from Kent, Sussex, Surrey, Essex, Somersetshire and Dorsetshire. The prices ran from £4 to £6 10s.; the larger dealers buying about fifty to sixty each, which they trucked (25 to 30 in a truck) away by rail.

One lot of about 55 were sold at once by auction at Brighton, and realized£6, £7 and £8 each, one fetching £10. The foals improve enormously on good keep. Our Forest feed is hardly good enough; on richer lands the ponies grow nearly a hand higher and get more substance.

Since our Association has improved the breed, of late years, very many have gone to the Kent Marshes, where they are highly thought of, very much more so than the Dartmoor ponies.

Yearlings at last Lyndhurst Pony Fair, in August, fetched £5 to £8, but the average was spoiled by two large sales by auction of 'lane haunters'—old mares and other cast-offs—which realized small prices.... I have seen some of our improved ponies at Hastings and elsewhere, broken in, and about five years old. They are much valued and sell for about £25.... The general improvement since 1889 or 1890 is very marked; and, though there was some opposition to the idea of bettering 'the real Forester' at first, now all admit the benefit of the work."

For the information of those interested in this breed, the following description, furnished to the Polo Pony Society for their Stud Book (Vol. V.) by the New Forest Local Committee, may be quoted:

For the New Forest pony, it is difficult to give any exact description, but the best class of them are from 12 hands to 13 hands 2 inches high according to the portion of the Forest on which they are reared.

If taken off the Forest when they are weaned and well-kept during the first two winters, they are said very often to attain the size of 14 hands 1 inch.

There is sometimes an apparent deficiency of bone, but what bone there is should be of the very best quality.

The feet are wide and well formed. They are often considered goose-rumped, but their hocks should be all that could be desired.

In color they may be said to range through every variety, though there are not many duns, and few if any piebalds left. The flea-bitten greys which are still very numerous on the Forest show strong traces of an Arabian cross.

The shoulders, though not always what might be desired in point of depth, are almost invariably fine and well laid.

And finally, it is a great characteristic of the New Forest pony to be always gay and alert, and, though they are extremely good-tempered and docile when fairly broken, they are really quite indomitable until they are completely cornered. The true Forester is never sulky.

A PONY HACK.

Engraved on wood by F. Babbage.

A pony well-known on Newmarket Heath and North Country racecourses about 1828.

CHAPTER 3

The Welsh Pony

At the period when Wales was an independent kingdom, livestock was protected by a singularly comprehensive series of laws. These were originally codified by Howel Dda (the Good), a prince who reigned from A.D. 942 to 948, and at a somewhat later period they were embodied in three distinct legal codes, the Venedotian, Dimetian and Gwentian, applicable respectively to North, South and South-eastern Wales, conforming to the local customs which prevailed in each area.

Under these laws, no Welsh serf was permitted to sell a stallion without the permission of his lord. The value of a horse—or, more accurately speaking, pony, as the hill ponies were the only equine stock the country possessed in those days—was laid down without regard to individual merit until he reached his third year. A foal until a fortnight old was worth four pence; from the fifteenth day of his age until one year old, 24 pence; when a year and one day old he was worth 48 pence and stood at that value until he began his third year when he was valued at 60 pence.

When in his third year, the pony was broken in, and his value depended on the work he was fitted for. A palfrey or sumpter horse was valued at 120 pence, and a working horse to draw cart or harrow 60 pence.

It was not permissible to use horses, mares, or cows for ploughing for fear of injury; only oxen might be employed for such labor. Any entire male animal was worth three females; thus, a wild stallion was worth nine score pence to the mare's value of three score pence.

If a horse were sold, he was to be warranted against staggers for three nights, against "black strangles" for three months, and against farcy for a year. (The commentators believe the disease so termed to be glanders; but inasmuch as the warranty against farcy held good for twelve months, perhaps we should accept this reading with reserve.)

He was to be warranted against restiveness until the purchaser should have ridden him three times "amid concourse of men and horses;" and if he proved restive the seller had to refund one third of the price he had received.

The value of each part of the horse was strictly specified by these laws. The worth of his foot was equal to his full value; each eye was esteemed worth one third of his full value. For every blemish in a horse, one third of the total worth was to be returned, his ears and tail included: a not obscure hint that cropping and docking were practiced in Wales at this period, and that opinions varied concerning the desirability of the operations.

That docking was in vogue is certain, for a special clause makes the "tail of a filly for common work" worth the total value of the animal. The peculiar value of the tail of a "filly for common work" lay in the fact that the harrow was often secured to the tail, as was the practice in parts of Ireland and Scotland until near the end of the last century.

In Wales, as in other parts of Britain, the mare was preferably used for draught and pack work, horses being reserved for military service. The mane and bridle were worth the same amount, that is to say, four pence; the forelock and halter were also coupled as worth one penny each.

Howel Dda's "Law of Borrowing" was equally comprehensive. The man who borrowed a horse and fretted the hair on his back was to pay four pence. If he broke the skin to the flesh, eight pence. And if skin and flesh were broken to the bone, sixteen pence were owed. Borrowing without the owner's leave was expensive: the borrower had to pay four pence for mounting, and four pence for each rhandir (supposed to be a league) he rode the horse. He also had to pay a fine to the owner's lord. If a hired horse fell lame or was injured by accident, the owner had to furnish the hirer with one equally good until the injured horse recovered. The laws which regulated compensation for trespass show that it was customary to fetter or clog the horses when they were turned out to graze. Trespass in corn by a clogged horse was to be compensated by payment of one penny by day, and two pence by night.

Trespass by a horse free of restraint was recompensed by half those sums. In this connection, it must be noted that stallions were "privileged;" and though a broken-in entire ran at large for three seasons (season from mid-April to mid-May as well as the month of October), he did not lose the privilege which relieved his owner from fines for any damage he might do in the standing crops.

The Welsh pony is more numerous than any other breed. He wanders over the hills and waste lands in all the twelve counties of the Principality, and also on the borders of Shropshire, Herefordshire and Monmouth; whereas his congeners are limited areas insignificant by comparison. The distribution is, of course, very unequal, the strength and number of droves varying with the character of the country.

There are no statistics in existence nor has there been made any estimate of their number.

Many of the common lands which were once open to the Welsh pony have been enclosed of recent years, but in spite of his exclusion from the better pastures and the warfare waged against him by shepherds and their dogs in the interests of grazing for sheep, he thrives marvelously. There are thousands of acres of wet and boggy lands whose grasses "rot" sheep, but which afford the hardy pony a nourishing diet.

In some districts, he is kept on the move almost as unceasingly as are the deer in Scotland or on Exmoor. And the life he leads has done much to develop his instincts of self-preservation.

Accustomed from earliest foalhood to the roughest ground, he is as sure-footed as the goat, and neither punishment nor persuasion will induce him to venture upon unsafe bog. He has good shoulders, strong back, a neat head and the most enduring legs and feet; he is, in short, a strong, sound and useful animal.

Some of the stoutest and best hunters bred on the borders of Wales trace their descent from the Welsh pony mare crossed with the thoroughbred sire; and the same may be said of some of the best modern steeplechasers.

J. C. Loudon, in his work, *An Encyclopedia of Agriculture*, published in 1825, writes:— "The Welsh horse bears a near resemblance in point of size to the best native breed of the Highlands of Scotland. It is too small for the two-horse ploughs; one that I rode for many years, which, to the last, would have gone upon a pavement by choice, in preference to a softer road."

Again, the celebrated sporting writer, "Nimrod" (C. J. Appleby), in his book *The Horse and the Hound*, published in 1842, writes of this breed as follows:—

> "They are never lame in the feet, or become roarers; they are also very little susceptible of disease in comparison with other horses, and as a proof also of their powers of crossing a country, the fact may be stated of the late Sir Charles Turner riding a pony ten miles in forty-seven minutes, and taking thirty leaps in his course, for a wager of 1,000 guineas, with the late Duke of Queensberry.... The Earl of Oxford had a mare pony, got by the Clive Arabian, her dam by the same horse, out of a Welsh mare pony, which could beat any of his racers four miles at a featherweight; and during the drawing of the Irish lottery the news was conveyed express from Holyhead to London chiefly by ponies, at the rate of nearly twenty miles an hour."

Endeavors have been made from time to time to improve the breed, but these efforts have been made by individuals, and the benefits, when any followed, were local and temporary.

The first recorded introduction of superior alien blood occurred in the first quarter of the eighteenth century, when that famous little horse, Merlin, was turned out to summer on the Welsh hills after his retirement from the Turf.

The small horses which George II's Act (p. 8) sought to banish from the racecourse were not all worthless; "vile and paltry" they may have been as a class, but there were some good ones among them, and Merlin was the best.

This little horse, who owed his name to the smallest of British hawks, beat every animal that started against him, and enjoyed a career of uninterrupted success until he broke down. Merlin was then purchased by a Welsh gentleman, said to have been an ancestor of Sir Watkin Williams Wynn, and turned out to run with the droves on the hills.

So remarkable was the improvement wrought upon the breed by this one stallion that in course of a few years the value of the ponies in that locality greatly increased. The name of the sire was applied to his stock and their descendants, which became famous as "Merlins." A certificate that proved an animal one of the true Merlin breed made all the difference in the market.

That usually accurate authority, Richard Berenger, in his *History and Art of Horsemanship* (published in 1771) says, the Welsh breed, "once so abundant, is now nearly extinct;" but in this he must have been mistaken, as there is evidence from the district to show that twenty-six years later, the Welsh pony was very, very far from extinct.

"A Farmer" writes to the *Gentleman's Magazine* in July 1797, complaining of the "injurious increase of the smallest breed of ponies, which are no kind of use," and which, he says, do an immense amount of mischief to the growing corn. The farmer ventured to assert that for every one cow found trespassing, ten ponies would be seen, and strongly urged that an Act of Parliament should be passed forbidding right of common to horses under 14 hands high.

In the middle of the present century, when fast-trotting animals for harness and saddle were in great demand, it was thought desirable to see what could be done with the Welsh pony, and accordingly Comet, Fire-away, Alonzo the Brave, and other fast-stepping small-sized Hackney sires were brought from Norfolk into Cardiganshire and Breconshire to cross with the native ponies. Such a cross could hardly have failed to result in a strong, fast-trotting and useful pony.

The Report issued by the recent Royal Commission on Land in Wales and Monmouthshire contains some relevant remarks on the subject which must be reproduced here:—

"With regard to cobs and ponies, breeding in this direction is a much larger factor in the farming of Wales. There is plenty of material to make use of, and the breeding of ponies might be made much more profitable than it is at present.

In the counties of Radnor and Brecon there has been some systematic attempts to encourage the breeding of cobs, with satisfactory results. On the mountains of North Wales, which were formerly famous for wild herds of Merlins, little has, however, been done.

Lord Penrhyn purchased an excellent stallion, Caradoc, who might have done much good had he been more patronized. The fault seems to lie in the careless treatment of the herds of ponies, which are allowed to ramble at will, winter and summer, to live or starve as nature may please. No attention whatever is paid to the breeding, the herds being wild to all intents and purposes. It seems a pity that such waste should be allowed.

The stoutness and endurance of the Welsh pony is proverbial, and if attention were paid to selection in breeding, separation of the sexes, and feeding and shelter in the winter, an exceedingly valuable addition to the mountain farmer's profits might be found at a small cost.

Turning to the evidence upon this subject: Mr. J. E. Jones, who appeared before us at Tregaron, gave it as his opinion that the breed of cobs was deteriorating; while Mr. Bowen Woosnam, of Tynygraig, near Builth, himself a successful breeder, stated that not nearly as much attention was paid to breeding cobs as formerly. Mr. Woosnam also said: If Welsh farmers were to have a portion of their money invested in ponies and cobs which are suitable to the farms that they are occupying, they would derive proportionately a larger income from them than they would from the cattle or sheep that they are rearing.... I do not mean to say that their stock should exclusively consist of ponies and cobs, but that they should have a few on every suitable farm. There is the greatest difficulty at the present time in getting good ponies and cobs."

The Commissioners were evidently unaware of the work which had been done by the Church Stretton Hill Pony Improvement Society. This society was formed to encourage and assist the farmers in the work of improving the ponies which they only too generally neglect.

The plan followed was to take up the best of the native stallions for service: those of the truest type only were used, and the improvement in the young stock got by these selected sires was marked. They showed more compactness of build, better bone, and greater spirit than their promiscuously bred brethren of the wilds.

There can be no doubt but that continuance of work on these lines would do much towards converting the scarcely saleable raw material of the Hills into profitable stock.

Mr. John Hill, of Marshbrook House, Church Stretton, in his attempts to breed polo ponies has shown that a valuable riding and harness animal can be obtained by judicious crossings of the Welsh pony.

Running more or less wild on the hills in the immediate neighborhood of Church Stretton are ponies closely allied to and very similar to the Welsh mountain breed. These usually range from 10 hands to 11 hands 2 inches in height, 12 hands 2 inches being considered the outside limit.

Around the year 1891, Mr. Hill purchased several of the best and most typical mares, wild and unbroken, from the hills. These mares, which averaged only 10 hands, were put to an Arab. His stock were handsome, compact and hardy, and grew to an average height of 13 hands.

The fillies of this cross when two years old were put to the best Welsh pony procurable, a 14-hand 1-inch stallion with riding shoulders and showing bone and quality.

These mares were subsequently put to a small thoroughbred, and to him threw foals full of quality and in every way promising. Mr. Hill's breeding experiments have all been made with the 14-hand 2-inch polo pony in view: and he has shown that Welsh ponies judiciously crossed with suitable alien blood produce stock for which a ready market should be found.

Mr. W. J. Roberts, the Hon. Secretary of the Church Stretton Hill Pony Society, states that he has tried the Arab cross, but "the offspring is useless on the hills."

A half-bred Arab is not the animal to successfully withstand the hardships and exposure of half-wild existence on the Welsh hills. The object sought in improving the Welsh or any other of these breeds is not to fit it for a life of semi-wildness but to make it more serviceable to man. For the information of those interested in this breed, the following descriptions, furnished to the Polo Pony Society for their Stud Book (Vol. V) by the Local Committees, may be quoted:

NORTH WALES DIVISION.

Height. *Not to exceed 12·2 hands.*

Color. *Bay or brown preferred; grey or black allowable; but dun, chestnut, or broken color considered objectionable.*

Action. *Best described as that of the hunter; low "daisy-cutting" action to be avoided. The pony should move quickly and actively, stepping out well from the shoulder, at the same time flexing the hocks and bringing the hind legs well under the body when going.*

General Character. *The pony should show good "pony" character and evidence of robust constitution, with the unmistakable appearance of hardiness peculiar to mountain ponies, and at the same time have a lively appearance.*

Head. *Should be small, well chiseled in its outline and well set on; forehead broad, tapering towards nose.*

Nostrils. *Large and expanding.* Eyes. *Bright, mild, intelligent and prominent.*

Ears. *Neatly set, well-formed and small.*

Throat and Jaws. *Fine, showing no signs of coarseness or throatiness.*

Neck. *Of proportionate length; strong, but not too heavy, with a moderate crest in the case of the stallion.*

Shoulders. *Good shoulders most important: should be well laid back and sloping, but not too fine at the withers nor loaded at the points. The pony should have a good long shoulder-blade.*

Back and Loins. *Strong and well covered with muscle.*

Hind Quarters. *Long, and tail well carried, as much like the Arab as possible, springing well from the top of the back.*

Hocks. *Well let down, clean cut, with plenty of bone below the joint. They should not be "sickled" or "cow-hocked."*

Forelegs. *Well placed; not tied in any way at the elbows; good muscular arm, short from the knee to the fetlock joints; flat bone; pasterns sloping but not too long; feet well developed and open at the heel; hoof sound and hard.*

SOUTH WALES DIVISION.

The South Wales hill pony seldom exceeds 13 hands, and in a pure state is about 12 hands. His attributes are a quick, straight action and sure-footedness; he is low in the withers, short in his forehand, and with faulty hind quarters as far as appearance goes, his tail being set on low and his hocks sickled, but his forelegs and feet are good. His head and eye show breed, courage and sense, and his constitution is strong or he could not live where he does. Of late years he has been crossed with the Cardiganshire cob to some extent; and half-bred two-year-old shire colts have been allowed access to the hills in summer in some places, much to the detriment of the breed. In color, bays and brown prevail.

The Welsh Pony today

CHAPTER 4

The Exmoor & Dartmoor Ponies

It is certain that ponies have run in these districts for many centuries in a practically wild state, and probably have always supplied the tillers of the soil with beasts of burden. In times when these localities were without roads of any kind and wheeled traffic was impossible, the sled and the packhorse were used for transporting agricultural produce.

The sleds were drawn by oxen and small horses; and ponies were employed to carry corn, and other things in pots and panniers. The ponies used for this purpose being the animals which ran at large upon the wastes.

As recently as 1860 packhorses might still be met with in the western and southern districts. They were the larger ponies of the Dartmoor and Exmoor breed, and were indispensable to the farmers whose holdings at that time lay beyond the region of roads in secluded districts.

The practice of taking up a few of the best mares for breeding purposes and keeping them in enclosed pasture is no doubt an old one; but the vast majority of the droves have always been left to their own devices. They bred and interbred without let or hindrance, and by consequence the weakly died off, leaving the fittest (the hardiest and the best able to withstand the rigors of exposure).

Carew, in his *History of Cornwall*, which was written in the early part of the reign of James I. (1603-1625), says:—

"The Cornish horses are hardly bred, coarsely fed, and so low in stature that they were liable to be seized on as unstatutable, according to the statute of Henry VIII., by anyone who caught them de-pasturing the commons."

In the year 1812 Exmoor was disforested by George III., and a commission was appointed to survey and value the lands. The total acreage was found to be 18,810 acres, of which 10,262 acres were adjudged the property of the Crown.

In 1820 Mr. John Knight purchased the Crown allotment; at a later date he acquired Sir Thomas Acland's portion, and Sir Arthur Chichester's property of Brendon which adjoined it, the total area so acquired being over 16,000 acres. Sir Thomas Acland had bred ponies, and when Mr. Knight bought the land, he applied himself to the task of improving the ponies, which for some years previously had been fetching only from £4 to £6.

The low prices obtainable, we infer, were due in a measure to the ease with which the local shepherds "took liberal tithe" of the ponies, which, despite the anchor-brand they bore to prove ownership, were readily purchased in Wiltshire.

The only pure Exmoor ponies now existing, so far as enquiry has disclosed, are those bred by Sir T. Dyke Acland, Bart., of Holnicote, Taunton.

When Sir Thomas Acland sold his Exmoor property to Mr. Knight, he removed his original uncrossed stock to Winsford Hill, near Dulverton. These ponies alone preserve the full characteristics of the old strain. They run from 11.2 hands to 12.2 hands, are dark brown with black points, and have the mealy tan muzzle. It is stated that only about a dozen mares were left in their old quarters.

Mr. Knight and some other gentlemen were attracted by the accounts of the Dongola Arab horses given by the great traveler Bruce, and after considerable delay, a number of stallions and mares were procured through the British Consul in Egypt.

They proved to be black, short-backed animals with lean heads, and rather Roman noses. Their hind quarters were good, but, unlike the typical Arab, they had "flattish ribs."

Mr. Knight became the owner of two sires and three mares, which he brought to Simonsbath. One of these Dongola stallions was mated with a number of 12-hand Exmoor mares. The foals generally grew to about 14 hands 2 inches, and though they followed their dams in the color of coat, the distinctive mealy muzzle disappeared. There was a desire to retain as much of the Exmoor character as was compatible with improvement in the breed, hence those half-bred mares by the Dongola horse which did not retain as much as possible of the native type were drafted from the stud.

The thoroughbred horse Pandarus, a 15-hand son of Whalebone, succeeded the Dongola horse. Foals of his get retained the original color, but were smaller, ranging from 13 hands to 13.2.

Another thoroughbred, Canopus, a grandson of Velocipede, followed Pandarus at the stud, and with equally satisfactory results in respect of improved size and conformation.

But, as might have been expected, these cross-bred ponies proved incapable of enduring the hardships of moorland life when turned out. Hence, about 1844, Mr. Knight gave up the use of alien blood and used his own stallion ponies; the only exceptions being Hero, a sturdy chestnut out of a Pandarus mare, and Lillias, a grey of nearly pure Acland strain.

After Mr. Knight's death, which event occurred in 1850, the practice of selling the ponies by private contract was abandoned in favor of an annual auction, held at Simonsbath. The comparative inaccessibility of the spot, however, soon indicated the need of change, and in 1854 the sale was first held at Bampton fair.

The system on which the ponies were kept was also changed in the later fifties; some 130 acres of pasture were set apart, and on this the foals were wintered instead of remaining at large on the bleak hillsides.

The effect thus produced upon the size and development of the young stock was very marked. In 1863, the ponies mustered about four hundred strong, nearly one hundred of which were brood mares, young and old. Much of the land which in former days was given up to the droves has been reclaimed during recent years, and improved methods of cultivation have made it capable of growing various crops and of grazing cattle and sheep.

Mr. Robert Smith, of Emmett's Grange, also devoted attention to the improvement of the Exmoor breed. The "Druid," who described a visit to Devonshire about the year 1860 or 1861, remarks that "the original color of the Exmoor seems to have been a buffy bay, with a mealy nose, and it is supposed to have preserved its character ever since the Phoenicians brought it over when they visited the shores of Cornwall to trade in tin and metals." Enquiry into the ground for supposing that the original stock was introduced by the Phoenicians would perhaps produce results hardly commensurate with the labor of research.

When the "Druid" paid his visit to the district in 1860 or 1861, only 250 acres of moorland remained unenclosed, and the breeding stock on Mr. Smith's holding consisted of "some twenty-five short-legged brood mares of about 13 hands 2 inches." These passed the better part of the year on the hills and were wintered in the paddocks furnished with open sheds for shelter.

After experimenting with thoroughbreds, Mr. Smith procured a 14-hand pony sire named Bobby, by Round Robin out of an Arab mare, and used him with the most encouraging results for two seasons.

Bobby's stock were almost invariably bays. At a sale held at Bristol, in 1864, twenty-nine cobs galloways and ponies, nearly all of which were Bobby's get, made an average price of 23 guineas a head, several realizing over 30 guineas. The highest price (figure not recorded) was paid for a bay stallion, five years old and 13 hands high.

Whether Youatt refers to the improved breed or not it is impossible to say: but that authority states that about the year 1860 a farmer who weighed 14 stone rode an Exmoor pony from Bristol to South Molton, a distance of 86 miles, beating the coach which travelled the same road. This feat proves the pony to have been both fast and enduring.

A most competent authority who a couple of years ago paid a visit to Simonsbath to inspect the ponies of the district, describes the "Acland" as a wonderfully thoroughbred looking and handsome pony with fine lean head, intelligent eye and good limbs. The only fault he had to find was in the matter of size: he considered it a shade too small for general purposes.

The "Knights" were described as larger than the "Aclands." They also retain the thoroughbred look derived from the Arab and other alien blood introduced by Mr. Knight in the second quarter of the century. My informant remarks that one of the most interesting sights he witnessed was the display of jealousy by the stallions when two droves of ponies were brought up for inspection. Each kept his harem crowded together apart from the other, "rounding in" his mares with the greatest fire. Needless to say, the little horses would show at their very best under such conditions.

Among the gentlemen who have endeavored to improve the Exmoor pony, mention must also be made of the Earl of Carnarvon, Viscount Ebrington and Mr. Nicholas Snow, of Oare, who have breeding studs; but their strains, like those of the farmers' who rear a few each, are larger than the representative "Aclands."

Dr. Herbert Watney, of Buckhold, near Pangbourne, until recently possessed herds of Exmoor and Arab-Exmoor ponies. Their numbers have quite lately been greatly reduced by the sale of mares and young stock, Dr. Watney holding the writer's view that ground in time becomes staled if grazed by numerous horses. (See my *Young Racehorses: Suggestions for Rearing* for more on this).

Dr. Watney laid the foundations of his herd by the purchase of about a dozen mares of the Knight and Ackland strains, and to serve them he acquired the 13.2 Exmoor stallion Katerfelto, winner of the first prize for pony stallions at the Devon County Show, and first prize in his class at the "Royal" in 1890.

The stallion runs with the mares, and the herd lead on the Berkshire downs exactly the same free life they led on Exmoor. They are never brought under cover, and only when snow buries the herbage in severe winters do they receive a daily ration of hay. The richer grazing and their exclusive service by Katerfelto has resulted in distinct increase of size, the ponies ranging from 11.3 to 13.3 in height, yet retaining all the characteristics of the Exmoor native stock.

Dr. Watney drafted off a number of the best mares to form a herd for service by the Arab pony stallion Nejram, a bay standing 14.1, bred by Mr. Wilford Blunt at Crabbet Park.

Nejram's stock show in marked degree the distinctive character of their sire in the high set and carriage of the tail, full barrel, blood-like head and the long pastern; but at the same time, they inherit from their dams the wonderful sure-footedness of the Exmoor pony. These ponies run from about 13 hands to 13.3.

Half a dozen of these Arab-Exmoors, three years old, handled but unbroken, were sold in the year 1898 at an average price of over £14 14s. each. Twelve pure Exmoors by Katerfelto, also handled but unbroken, three years old, brought an average of over £16 16s.

Bampton Fair, held in October, is now the great rendezvous for Exmoor ponies. Every fair brings several hundred animals in from the moors for sale. Like other horses and ponies, the Exmoors are suffering from the competition of the bicycle, but good prices are still obtained under the hammer.

They are much used for children, and the less desirable find ready sale to coster-mongers and hawkers. Newly weaned suckers of five- or six-months old fetch from £3 to £6; exceptionally promising youngsters command a higher figure.

The Dartmoor pony's good points are a strong back and loin, and substance. For generations past, the farmers appear to have been in the habit of taking up a few mares for riding and breeding purposes; to these 11 or 12-hand dams—they rarely reach 13 hands—a small Welsh cart stallion is put, and the result is an animal hardy and serviceable enough for ordinary farm work. Even these would seem to form a small minority.

For the most part the Dartmoor ponies still run wild, shaggy and unkempt, on the waste lands on which they breed uncontrolled, on which they are foaled and live and die; often without having looked through a bridle. Those taken up for riding purposes or for breeding are, of course, the pick of the droves, and thus we find an active force at work which is calculated to lower the average standard of quality among the wild ponies.

In considering the various efforts which from time to time have been made in the direction of improvement by the introduction of fresh blood, we must bear in mind that the mares on which such experiments have been made are those which have been taken up by farmers and kept within fences.

We cannot find that stallions of alien blood have ever been turned out to run on the moors, and in view of the conditions under which the moor ponies exist it is highly improbable that a stallion boasting such blood as would produce beneficial results on the native breed would long enough survive the exposure and scanty food to make any appreciable mark thereon.

The endeavors, more or less continuous and successful, to improve the breed have been confined to the few, and have, therefore, produced little effect or none on the main stock.

Early in the present century Mr. Willing, of Torpeak, made successful experiments in crossing the Exmoor pony with the smaller variety peculiar to the Dartmoor "tors."

Mr. Wooton, of Woodlands, says a writer in the *Field* of 9th October, 1880, was in the habit of purchasing mares of this cross from Mr. Willing from about the year 1820, and possessed a considerable number of them. He used to put these to small thoroughbred horses standing in the district. The names of Trap, Tim Whiffler, Rover, and Glen Stuart are mentioned, and in about 1860 he sent some of his Exmoor-Dartmoor mares to a small Arab belonging to Mr. Stewart Hawkins, of

Ivybridge. Mr. Wooton's endeavors to improve the Dartmoor breed are the first that were made on any considerable scale, so far as it is possible to discover.

About 1879, a resident who devoted much attention to the improvement of the Dartmoor breed introduced a brown stallion by Mr. Christopher Wilson's Sir George out of Windsor Soarer, and as his mares—a selected lot, 12.2 to 13 hands, either brown or chestnut—came in use, put them to this pony with the object of getting early foals.

The young stock thus got were carefully weeded out, the best stallions and mares only being retained. The colt foals were kept apart and at two years old put to the mares got by their sire. The experiment was very successful, browns, black-browns and chestnuts being the colors of this improved breed, which sold well.

Mr. S. Lang, of Bristol, some years prior to 1880 sent down two good stallions, Perfection and Hereford, for use in the district, but it is stated that these ponies were little patronized by the farmers. Hereford, a pure thoroughbred pony who was only 13 hands high, left a few beautiful foals behind him.

A description of Exmoor and Dartmoor ponies exhibited at the Newton Abbott Agricultural Show in May of 1875 may have had reference to these improved ponies. The following is quoted from the *Field* of 29th May in that year:—

"Instead of deteriorating the stock improves yearly, and the care which is now taken to infuse pure blood without harming the essential characteristics of the original denizen of the moor has succeeded in producing an animal of superlative merit, fitted for any kind of work, whether for the field, the road, or the collar.

It must be observed that the word 'moor' should apply to Exmoor and the Bodmin wastes as well as the Forest of Dartmoor, Dartmoor Forest itself being within the precincts of the Duchy of Cornwall.

The moor pony or galloway of 14 hands is often in reality a little horse; and when it is stated that Tom Thumb, the well-known hunter of Mr. Trelawny, was a direct descendant of the celebrated Rough Tor pony of Landue, and that Foster by Gainsborough, belonging to the late Mr. Phillips, of Landue, carrying for many years fifteen stone and upwards in the first flight, was from a moor pony near Ivybridge, the assertion is not made without bringing strong collateral proof of the validity of the statement.

Moreover, a host of other examples could be added. These animals possess many of the properties of the thoroughbred—speed, activity, any amount of stay, with legs of steel; they can jump as well as the moor sheep, and much after the same fashion, for no hedge fence can stop either one or the other."

For the information of those interested in this breed the following descriptions furnished to the Polo Pony Society for their Stud Book (vol. v.) by Local Committees may be quoted:

THE EXMOOR DIVISION

The official Exmoor pony:—
Height. *Should average 12 hands and never be above 13 hands; moorland bred.*

Color: *generally dark bay or brown with black points.*

Head. *Wide forehead and nostril; mealy nose; sharp ears.*

Shape. *Good shoulders & back; short legs, with good bone & fair action.*

Note: There are a few grey ponies in Sir Thomas Acland's herd, but no chestnuts.

THE DARTMOOR DIVISION

The official description of points is identical with that given for the North Wales pony, with the following amendments and additions:—

Height. *Not exceeding 14 hands for stallions, 13·2 for mares.*

Color. *Brown, black, or bay preferred; grey allowable, other colors objectionable.*

Head. *Should be small, well set on, and blood-like.*

Neck. *Strong but not too heavy, and neither long nor short; and, in case of a stallion, with moderate crest.*

Back, Loins, & Hind Quarters. *Strong and well covered with muscle.*

This Dartmoor foal is having a grand time.

CHAPTER 5

Cumberland & Westmoreland Ponies

The ponies and galloways, for which the wastelands of these counties have long been known, appear to possess no distinguishing characteristics that would permit it to be said they form a distinct breed.

An authority resident at Harrington who gives much information concerning the ponies of the heafs—fell-side holdings—and moors, states that there are several strains, and the appearance and character of each differs in various districts under the varying local influences of climate, feed, etc.

Little or nothing is known of the origin of these ponies. The resemblance to "Shelties," borne by those of certain localities until about the middle of the century, suggested that they were descended from a mixed stock of galloways and Shetland ponies. But some forty or fifty years ago, efforts were made to improve them by careful selection and mating; and the resemblance, which did not necessarily imply possession of the merits of the Shetland pony, has in great measure disappeared.

They are generally good-tempered; so sure-footed that they can gallop down the steep hillsides with surprising speed and fearlessness. But their paces on level ground are not fast.

Their endurance has been remarked by many writers. Brown's *Anecdotes and Sketches of the Horse*, published about sixty years ago, contains an account of an extraordinary performance by a galloway, at Carlisle, in 1701 when a Mr. Sinclair, of Kirkby Lonsdale, for a wager of 500 guineas, rode the animal 1000 miles in 1000 hours.

The ponies run in "gangs" on the holdings, the gang numbering from half a dozen to forty or even sixty individuals. In some cases, a few ponies are taken up, broken and worked all the year round, carrying the farmer to market, drawing peat and hay, and ploughing.

The stony nature of the heaf-lands requires only a light plough, which is easily drawn by one or two of the half-pony, half-horse nondescripts. The extent of arable land farmed by any one farmer is only from four to six acres.

A stallion is sometimes used for the farm-work, and in such cases the neighboring farmers bring mares to be served. Some such stallions will serve from thirty to fifty mares in the season. In the larger gangs the stallion runs with the mares on the hills.

A good breeding mare often lives and dies without knowing a halter, running practically wild from the day she is dropped on the fell-side till she dies. These unhandled ponies pick up their living on the hills, and during winter a little hay is brought out to them by the shepherds.

The "Fell-siders," as the holders of heafs are called locally, make no attempt to improve their wild pony stock; under the existing conditions the wild mares drop their foals, it may be without the knowledge of their owner. Farmers who bring their mares to a neighbor's working stallion exercise no discrimination in their choice; the cheapest and most accessible horse receives their preference.

Where skill and judgment have been brought to bear upon the improvement of the Fell ponies, the result has been very marked. Mr. Christopher W. Wilson, of Rigmaden Park, Kirkby Lonsdale, Westmoreland, was the pioneer of an improved breed of ponies, and he has shown what can be done with the material at hand, having built upon that foundation a breed which at the present day stands unrivalled for shape and action.

Having in the year 1872 taken the matter in hand, Mr. Wilson selected his breeding mares from among the best ponies of the districts, and put them to the pony stallion, Sir George, a Yorkshire-bred Hackney—by Sportsman and by Prickwillow, descended through Phenomenon from the Original Shales—which won the first prizes for eight years straight at the Shows of the Royal Agricultural Society.

The female offspring were in due time mated with their sire and threw foals which showed Hackney characteristics in far more marked degree than did their dams, as might be anticipated in animals three-parts instead of one-half bred.

The chief difficulty Mr. Wilson had to contend with was the tendency of these ponies to exceed the 14 hands which is the limit of the pony classes at the shows.

This was overcome by turning out the young stock after the first winter upon the rabbit warrens and moorlands of Rigmaden to find their own grazing among the sheep and rabbits as their maternal ancestors had done.

This measure not only succeeded in its direct object but went far to preserve that hardiness of constitution which is by no means the least valuable attribute of the mountain pony.

This judicious system of breeding and management was maintained with the best results; the third direct cross from Sir George produced a mare in Georgina V. which had constitution and stamina, and also more bone than her dam or grand dam. The breeder's name has been given to the fruits of his wisely directed efforts, and the "Wilson pony" is now universally famous for its hunter-like shape and action, and for the numerous successes it has achieved at the principal shows at home and abroad.

Mr. Wilson won the Queen's Jubilee gold medals for both stallions and mares at the Royal Agricultural Society's Show at Windsor and sold the stallion for a large sum to go to America. On one occasion the R.A.S.E. Show included three classes for pony stallions and three prizes in each. Well, Mr. Wilson entered nine ponies and won all these prizes; also 1st and 2nd prizes for pony brood mares.

Sir Humphrey de Trafford, Bart., was also most successful in producing ponies from stock purchased from Mr. Christopher Wilson. At the Flordon Sale, Norfolk, held in September, 1895, Sir Humphrey disposed of his large stud, when some of the ponies realized prices which are worth quoting: Snorer II., a brown mare, 13.3, eight years old, by Sir George—Snorer—Sir George, 600 gs.; Georgina V., a bay mare, 14 hands, six years old, by Sir George—Georgina II., Sir George—Georgina—Sir George, 700 gs.; Dorothy Derby, a bay mare, 14 hands, eight years old, by Lord Derby II.—Burton Agnes, 600 gs.; Dorothy Derby II., a bay mare, 14 hands, six years old, by Little II.—Dorothy Derby, 720 gs.; Snorter II., bay filly, two years old, by Cassius—Snorer II. by Sir George—Snorer—Sir George, 700 gs., and Miss Sniff, bay yearling filly, by Cassius—Snorer II., 900 gs.; the average for these six lots being no less than £756.

It is true that Sir Humphrey had spared neither money nor labor in founding the Flordon stud, and the ponies were animals of exceptional merit. Their high quality had won them prizes at all the principal shows in England, and their fame was literally "world-wide."

Twenty years ago, the late Rev. J. M. Lowther, rector of Boltongate, made an attempt on a modest scale to improve the ponies of the Caldbeck Fells by selecting sires and dams from among the best of them.

Two or three ponies of his breeding won prizes at Whitehaven and Carlisle; his best sire was a 13-hand pony named Mountain Hero. This little animal had splendid bone and was as hardy as the wildest of his kin. The picture here given is a portrait of Little Wonder II., the property of the Marquis of Londonderry. He was bred by Mr. Christopher W. Wilson, his sire being Little Wonder I., and his dam Snorer by Sir George.

Mr. William Graham, of Eden Grove, Kirkbythorpe, Penrith, writes:—

"Up to about twenty years ago, great interest seems to have been taken in pony or galloway cob breeding throughout the whole district of the Eden valley in the villages and hamlets that lie scattered all along the foot of the Pennine range of hills.

Previous to the days of railway transit the ponies and small galloway cobs were employed in droves as pack horses, as well as for riding, and many men now living can remember droves of from twenty to thirty continually travelling the district, carrying panniers of coal and other merchandise between the mines and villages.

The village of Dufton, in which the hill farm of Keisley is situated, was quite a center of pony breeding, and for many generations the Fell-side farmers in this district have been noted for their ponies; they bred them to the best Fell pony stallions, most of which were trained trotters of great speed.

Each of the three mares originally purchased to found the stud at Keisley were got from well-known locally bred dams and grand-dams, and all were selected to match each other in character and style.

The mare from which two of them were bred was from a very old strain by a stallion pony called Long Cropper, a record trotter; and all the three mares were themselves by a pony called Blooming Heather, another well-known pony stallion of a few generations younger.

These mares have been put to a stallion got by Mars from a pony mare belonging to Col. Stirling, Kippendavie, and the present stud, with the exception of two of the mares originally purchased, are all by him.

Last season, and this, a pony stallion by Little Wonder II. has been in use, and five or six of the mares have foaled to him, the end of May and beginning of June being quite early enough for these mares to foal, as they are never under cover unless broken-in, especially as they very readily stand to their service at first season after foaling.

When safe in foal they are turned out to the higher allotments and the open fell with their foals, where they run from July to November; save in exceptionally hard winters they get no hand feeding in the shape of hay, as they thrive and do well in the rough open allotments, to which they are generally brought down in November to remain until the end of March.

In height these ponies run from 12 to 13 hands, and with the exception of two blacks all are of uniform rich dark bay color with black points.

Just at first, when brought in wild to break, they are a little nervous, but if kindly treated soon become very docile and easily handled. They are very easily broken both for riding and driving, and ponies comparatively quite small carry with ease men of ordinary stature.

They are the most useful means of locomotion in crossing the mountain ranges and traversing the hilly roads of the district.

Although of no great size these ponies are very muscular, their bones and joints are fine, hard and clean, and, generally speaking, they have good middles. Some are perhaps a little short in quarter, but with a fair shoulder, and their legs, ankles and feet are all that can be desired.

There certainly seems to be very fair field in the district for breeding ponies, as they are very cheaply and easily reared, and when fit to break in can be disposed of for a very fairly good figure."

The Cumberland "Fell-siders" are wedded to the customs and usages of their ancestors, and endeavors to promote schemes for the general improvement of the ponies have met with small success.

Colonel Green-Thompson, of Bridekirk, Cockermouth, in 1897, offered the farmers the opportunity of using an Arab stallion, but the chance of thus bettering their stock appears to have been neglected by the breeders.

This is to be regretted, for the fells and dales offer thousands of acres of good, sound grazing land which might be far more profitably devoted to pony-breeding than given up to the few scattered flocks of Herdwick sheep which they now carry.

The sheep farmers of Caldbeck and Matterdale in Cumberland pay some attention to the business, asserting that the ponies are less trouble and involve less risk than sheep.

Their fillies are put to the horse at two years old, and they frequently obtain a second foal before sending the dam to market.

The colts command a readier sale than the mares.

The ordinary Fell pony, outside the district, is in demand for pit work, for which purpose suitable animals bring from £12 to £15.

Mr. W. W. Wingate-Saul supplies the following description of the Fell ponies:—

> "A very powerful and compact cobby build, the majority having a strong middle piece with deep chest and strong loin characteristics, which, combined with deep sloping shoulders and fine withers, make them essentially weight-carrying riding ponies.
>
> The prevailing—indeed, the only—colors are black, brown, bay, and, quite occasionally, grey. I do not remember ever having seen a chestnut, and if I found one I should think it due to the introduction of other blood.
>
> The four colors prevail in the order named, the best animals often being get black and usually without white markings, unless it be a small white star.
>
> The head is pony-like and intelligent, with large bright eyes and well-placed ears. The neck in the best examples being long enough to give a good rein to the rider. The hind quarters are square and strong, with a well-set-on tail. The legs have more bone than those of any of our breeds; ponies under 14 hands often measuring 8-1/2 inches below the knee. Their muscularity of arm, thigh and second thigh is marvelous.

Their habitat (having been bred for centuries on the cold inhospitable Fells, where they are still to be found) has caused a wonderful growth of hair, the winter coat being heavy and the legs growing a good deal of fine hair, all of which, excepting some at the point of the heel, is cast in summer.

Constitutionally they are tough as iron, with good all-round action, and are very fast and enduring."

S. Clark, Hallgarth, Photo.

LITTLE WONDER II.

CHAPTER 6

Ireland's Connemara Pony

Richard Berenger, Gentleman of the Horse to King George III in his work, *The History and Art of Horsemanship*, 1771—says that—

> "Ireland has for many centuries boasted a race of horses called Hobbies, valued for their easy paces and other pleasing and agreeable qualities, of a middling size, strong, nimble, well molded and hardy....
>
> The nobility have stallions of great reputation belonging to them, but choose to breed for the *Turf* in preference to other purposes; for which, perhaps, their country is not so well qualified, from the moisture of the atmosphere, and other causes, which hinder it from improving that elastic force and clearness of wind; and which are solely the gifts of a dry soil, and an air more pure and refined.
>
> This country, nevertheless, is capable of producing fine and noble horses."

The great stud maintained in England by Edward III. (1327-1377) included a number of Hobbies which were procured from Ireland. A French chronicler named Creton, who wrote a *Metrical History of the Deposition of Richard II.*, refers with great admiration to the Irish horses of the period.

He evidently accompanied King Richard during his expedition to Ireland in the summer of 1399, for he says the horses of that country "scour the hills and valleys fleeter than deer;" and he also states that the horse ridden by Macmore, an Irish chieftain, "without housing or saddle was worth 400 cows."

At a much later date the character of this breed was changed by the introduction of Spanish blood. Tradition asserts that the ponies which inhabited the rough and mountainous tracts of Connemara, in the county Galway, were descended from several animals that were saved from the wreck of a ship of the Spanish Armada in 1588.

It is, however, quite needless to invoke the aid of a somewhat too frequently employed a tradition to explain the character which at one period distinguished these ponies. Spanish stallions were freely imported into England from the fourteenth to seventeenth centuries, and it is probable that the character of the Connemara pony was derived not from shipwrecked stock but in a far more prosaic fashion: by importation of sires from England.

The testimony of many old writers goes to prove the high esteem in which Spanish horses were held. The Duke of Newcastle, in his famous work on *Horses and Horsemanship*, written in 1658, says:

> "I have had Spanish horses in my own possession which were proper to be painted after, or fit for a king to mount on a public occasion. Genets have a fine lofty air, trot and gallop well. The best breed is in Andalusia, especially that of the King of Spain at Cordova."

The Spanish horse of those times owed much to the Barbs, which were originally introduced into the country by the Moors; and if the Connemara pony was permitted to revert to the original type, something was done to re-establish the Spanish—or, perhaps, it is more accurate to go a step further back and say the "Barb"—character in the early thirties.

Mr. Samuel Ussher Roberts, C.B., in course of evidence given before the Royal Commission on Horse Breeding in Ireland in 1897, stated that he lived for five-and-twenty years in the west of Galway, and when in that part of the country, "there was," he said,

> "an extremely hardy, wiry class of pony in the district show-ing a great deal of the Barb or Arab blood. Without exception they were the best animals I ever knew—good shoulders, good hard legs, good action, and great stamina ... they were seldom over 14.2 hands. I never knew one of them to have a spavin or splint, or to be in any respect unsound in his wind.... There was a strong trace of Arab blood which I always understood arose from the introduction into Connemara of the Barb or Arab by the Martin family many years ago—you could very easily trace it to the Connemara ponies at the time I speak of."

In answer to a subsequent question, Mr. Ussher Roberts fixed the date of the introduction of the Barb or Arab blood by Colonel Martin at about 1833.

The old stamp of the Connemara pony was described by another witness, Mr. R. B. Begley, as "long and low with good rein, good back, and well coupled." But the majority of witnesses from Galway, and those who had personal knowledge of the breed, shared Mr. Ussher Roberts' opinion that it had greatly deteriorated since the middle of the century when the influence of the Barb or Arab sires had died out.

The young animals, it was stated, were collected in droves when about six months old, and hawked about the country for sale, bringing prices ranging from thirty shillings to £3. Many of these were purchased for use in the English coal pits.

Evidence was forthcoming to show that there are still some good specimens of the breed. Mr. John Purdon described a drove he had re-cently seen in Connemara: "They were beautiful mares, I never saw lovelier mares; about twenty in the drove, and foals with them. They were the perfect type of a small thoroughbred mare." These animals were the property of Mr. William Lyons, who kept a special breed for generations.

The falling off in quality was generally attributed to promiscuous breeding and to in-breeding. "In some parts of Connemara," said Mr. H. A. Robinson, "they just turn a stallion out loose on the mountains, mongrels of the very worst description."

There is, however, another factor in the loss of quality, namely, the terrible straits to which the peasantry were reduced in the time of the famine. A correspondent informs me that in south-west Cork, in the fifties, nearly all the people had mare ponies; in west Galway in the sixties there was scarcely an ass in Connemara west of Spiddal and Oughterard; and the case in west Mayo was the same.

When my informant visited the same districts fifteen or twenty years later, he observed a remarkable change. "Hard times" had come upon the people in the interim, and all the small holders had donkeys instead of ponies. Poverty had obliged them to sell their mares.

And when times improved, they were too impoverished to buy new ponies, and replaced them with asses.

Under such circumstances, of course, the better the mare owned by the peasant the more likely it was to find a purchaser; and little but the "rag, tag and bobtail" was left to perpetuate the species.

However considerably the remainder depreciated in quality, they still retained their characteristic hardiness of constitution and the germs of those qualities which under better auspices gained the breed its reputation.

Some of the witnesses who gave evidence before the Royal Commission mentioned experiments in cross breeding which prove how well and rapidly the Connemara pony responds to endeavor to improve it by the introduction of suitable fresh blood.

Mr. Samuel Johnston stated that he had bred one of the best hunters he ever possessed out of a Connemara mare; and Mr. R. B. Begley described a mare got by the pure-bred Hackney sire Star of the West from a "mountainy pony."

This Hackney-Connemara cross could cover an English mile in three minutes. Mr. Begley had driven her fifty-six Irish (over seventy-one statute) miles in a day and had repeatedly driven her twelve Irish (over fifteen statute) miles in an hour and ten minutes. He had won two prizes with her for action in harness at the Hollymount Show and had hunted her with ten stone on her back. With hounds as in the shafts this truly remarkable pony proved herself able to go and stay, performing well across country.

These Connemara ponies stand from 12 hands to 14 hands or more.

Like other breeds which run practically wild in mountainous country, they are above all things hardy, active and sure-footed: in response to the climatic conditions of their habitat—the climate of West Galway is the most humid of any spot in Europe—they grow a thick and shaggy coat which is very usually chestnut in color betraying their descent.

And although, yes, they have lost in size owing to the conditions of their existence and are rounder in the croup, they retain the peculiar ambling gait which distinguished their Spanish ancestors.

Those with whose breeding care has been taken, such as the drove belonging to Mr. William Lyons, of Oughterard, show the characteristics implanted by the infusion of Barb blood in their blood-like heads and clean limbs. Even those which have suffered through promiscuous breeding conform in their ugliness and shortcomings to the original type.

For some years past systematic endeavors to improve the breed have been in progress. The Congested Districts Board, under the Land Commission of Ireland, introduced small Hackney stallions whose substance, action, and robust constitution render them particularly well adapted to correct the defects of weedy and ill-shaped mares without impairing their natural hardiness.

The Connemara today: Grey mare. Galway, Ireland

CHAPTER 7

Scotland & Shetland Island Ponies

The Scottish nation from early times have possessed a breed of horses which was held in great esteem; and, as in England, laws were passed from time to time prohibiting their export from the country.

The second parliament of James I. in the year 1406 enacted (cap. 31) that no horse of three years old or under should be sent out of Scotland.

In 1567, James VI. Forbade the export of horses in an Act (Jac. VI., cap. 22) whose preface makes specific reference to Bordeaux, from which place there was a great demand for horses.

In a curious old book entitled *The Horseman's Honour* or the *Beautie of Horsemanship*, published in the year 1620 by an anonymous writer, we find the following passage:—

> "For the horses of Scotland they are much less than those of England, yet not inferior in goodness; and by reason of their smallness they keep few stoned but geld many by which likewise they retaine this saying 'That there is no gelding like those in Scotland,' and they, as the English, are for the most part amblers.
>
> Also in Scotland there are a race of small nagges which they call galloways or galloway nagges, which for fine shape easie pace, pure mettall and infinit toughnesse are not short of the best nagges that are bred in any countrey whatsoever; and for sound-

nesse in body they exceede the most races that are extant, as daily experience shews in their continual travels journeyings and fore-huntings."

In Berenger's "The History and Art of Horsemanship," he writes:

"This kingdom (Scotland) at present encourages a fleet breed of horses, and the nobility and gentry have many foreign and other stallions of great value in their possession with which they cultivate the breed and improve it with great knowledge and success.

Like the English they are fond of racing and have a celebrated course at Leith which is honored with a royal plate given by his present Majesty George III.

The wisdom and generosity likewise of the nobility and gentry have lately erected a riding house in the City of Edinburgh at their own expense and fixed a salary upon the person appointed to direct it.

This kingdom has been famous for breeding a peculiar sort of horses called Galloways. From the care and attention paid at present to the culture of horses it is to be expected that it will soon be able to send forth numbers of valuable and generous breeds destined to a variety of purposes and equal to all: the country being very capable of answering the wishes of the judicious breeder who need only remember that colts require to be well nourished in winter and sheltered from the severity of a rigorous and changeable sky."

The Galloway, so called from the part of Scotland known by that name, is a diminutive horse resembling the Welsh cob, to which the author of an *Encyclopedia of Agriculture* compares it in a passage quoted on a former page.

The breed gradually diminished in number as the advances of law and order deprived the moss-troopers and other predatory border men of a method of livelihood which involved the use of hardy and enduring horses.

Before the commencement of the nineteenth century and during more recent years this animal, which cannot be described either as a horse or a pony, has played an active part in agricultural work on the lowlands of Scotland.

In localities where no roads existed, and wheeled traffic was impossible, galloways were used not only for riding but for the transport of agricultural produce; as they lacked the weight and strength to draw the two-horse plough, ploughing was done by oxen, but the sledges which held the place of carts and wagons were drawn by the galloways, which were also used to carry corn and general merchandise in pots and panniers.

In height the original Galloway was generally under 14 hands. Youatt (second edition, 1846) describes it as from 13 to 14 hands, and sometimes more; it was a bright bay or brown, with black legs and small head.

The purposes for which it was used indicated the desirability of increasing its height and strength, and with this end in view cross breeding was commenced in the early part of the century and continued until so late a date as 1850. By consequence, the old Galloway has now almost disappeared from all parts of the mainland and survives only in such remote situations as the Island of Mull.

About the end of the eighteenth century a Mr. Gilchrist employed on his farm in Sutherlandshire as many as ten "garrons" to carry peats from the hills and seaweed from the shore. These burdens were carried in crates or panniers.

As Creech writes in his wonderful 1784 text *Husbandry in Scotland,*

"The little creatures do wonders; they set out at peep of day and never halt till the work of the day be finished—going 48 miles."

At the present time the most conspicuous field of utility open to the Scottish pony is that offered by the grouse-moors and deer-forests, though in the close season general farm and draught work affords them employment. A pony of from 13 to 14 hands may be strong enough for a man of average weight to ride on the grouse-moor; but for deer-stalking a sturdy cob of from 14 to 15 hands is necessary, a smaller animal is not equal to the task of carrying a heavy man or a 17-stone stag over the rough hills and valleys among which his work lies.

The origin of the "Sheltie," like that of the other breeds considered in the foregoing pages, is unknown. Mr. James Goudie, whose essay on *The Early History of the Shetland Pony* is published in the first volume of the *Shetland Pony Stud Book* thinks there is every likelihood that it was brought to the islands from Scotland at some very early period.

The "Bressay Stone," a sculptured slab which was discovered in Bressay in 1864, bears, among other designs in low relief, the figure of a horse on which a human figure is seated. "As this monument is admitted by authorities on the subject to belong to a period before the Celtic Christianity of the islands disappeared under the shock of Norwegian invasion [A.D. 872], it may be inferred ... that the animal was known and probably found in the islands at this period."

Early writers state that the Scandinavian invaders introduced the foundation stock some time prior to the fifteenth century. Buchanan makes passing reference to the Orkney and Shetland ponies in his *History of Scotland*, written three centuries ago: but the first description which has completeness to recommend it is that of Brand, who visited the islands in 1700 and wrote *A Brief Description of Orkney, Zetland, Pightland, Firth and Caithness*, which was published at Edinburgh in the following year. This author writes:—

"They are of a less size than the Orkney Horses, for some will be but 9, others 10 nives or hand-breadths high, and they will be thought big Horses there if 11, and although so small yet they are full of vigor and life, and some not so high as others often prove to be the strongest....

Summer or winter they never come into an house but run upon the mountains, in some places in flocks; and if any time in Winter the storm be so great that they are straitened for food they will come down from the Hills when the ebb is in the sea and eat the sea-ware ... which Winter storms and scarcity of fodder puts them out of ease and bringeth them so very low that they recover not their strength till St. John's Mass-day, the 24th of June, when they are at their best.

They will live to a considerable age, as twenty-six, twenty-eight or thirty years, and they will be good riding horses in twenty-four, especially they'll be the more vigorous and live the longer if they be four years old before they be put to work.

Those of a black color are judged to be the most durable and the pyeds often prove not so good; they have been more numerous than they now are."

Bengie, in his *Tour in Shetland* (1870), after remarking on their sure-footedness and hardiness of constitutions, suggests that the sagacity, spirit and activity for which they are remarkable may be due to the freedom of the life they live on the hills. He wrote:

"They are sprightly and active as terriers, sure-footed as mules and patient as donkeys."

They stand, he adds, at the head of the horse tribe as the most intelligent and faithful of them all; and he compares the intelligence of the Sheltie with that of the Iceland pony much to the advantage of the former. "Shorter in the leg than any other kind," says Mr. Robert Brydon, of Seaham Harbour, "they are at the same time wider in the body and shorter in the back, with larger bones, thighs and arms; and therefore, are comparatively stronger and able to do with ease as much work as average ponies of other breeds a hand higher."

The Shetland Stud Book Society will register no pony whose height exceeds 10 hands 2 inches, and the average height may be taken as 10 hands: many do not exceed 9 hands, and a lady who wrote an account of a visit to Shetland in 1840 speaks of one reared by Mr. William Hay, of Hayfield, which was only 26 inches, or 6 hands 2 inches high!

It is, however, unusual to find a pony measuring less than 8 hands at the shoulder, and we may perhaps doubt whether the 26-inch specimen was full-grown.

In color the Shetlander varies: bays, browns and dullish blacks are most common: sometimes these hues are relieved by white markings and occasionally white specimens occur: piebalds are rare. The coat in winter is long, close and shaggy, fit protection against the inclemency of the weather the pony endures without cover or shelter: in spring the heavy winter coat is shed, and in the summer months the hair is short and sleek.

In former times it was customary to hobble the ponies; but this practice, which must have done much to spoil their naturally good action, has been abandoned for many years.

It is now usual to give the ponies a ration of hay in the winter months when the vegetation is covered deep with snow, and thus the losses by starvation, which formerly were heavy in severe winters, are obviated.

Otherwise, the Sheltie's conditions of life to-day differ little from those that prevailed three centuries ago. Mr. Meiklejohn, of Bressay, states that in April, generally, the crofters turn their ponies out upon the common pasture lands, and leave them to their own devices. On common pastures where there are no stallions the mares are caught for service and tethered until the foal is born and can follow freely, when mother and child are turned out again.

In autumn when crops have been carried the ponies come down from the hills to their own townships, where they feed on the patches of fresh grass which have been preserved round the cultivated areas.

The nights being now cold, they remain in the low-lying lands sheltering under the lee of the yard walls; and "when winter has more fully set in the pony draws nearer his owner's door, and in most cases is rewarded with his morning sheaf on which, with seaweed and what he continues to pick off the green sward, the hardy animal manages to eke out a living until the time rolls round again that he is turned on the hill pasture, never being under a roof in his life."

At one period the ponies were apparently regarded almost as public property; for, among the "Acts and Statutes of the Lawting Sheriff and Justice Courts of Orkney and Shetland," was one passed in the year 1612 and frequently renewed, which forbade the "ryding ane uther manis horse without license and leave of the awner," under penalty of fine; and also provided that "quhasoever sall be tryet or fund to stow or cut ane uther man's hors taill sall be pwinischit as a theif at all rigour in exempill of utheris to commit the lyke."

The number of ponies on the islands has decreased in recent years by reason of the steadily growing demand from without. The latest available Government returns are those of 1891, and for the sake of comparison the returns of 1881 are given below:—

	1881	1891
Horses as returned by occupiers of land used solely for agriculture	921	787
Unbroken horses / mares kept solely for breeding	4323	4016

The ponies are little used for farm work in the Shetlands; they carry loads of peat from the hills to the crofts, and apart from this are used only for riding; they are beyond question the most wonderful weight-carriers in the world, a 9-hand pony being able to carry with the greatest ease a full-grown man over bad ground and for long distances.

They owe their value to the combination of minuteness and strength, which renders them peculiarly suitable for draught work in the coal mines. Many ponies will travel thirty miles a day, to and fro in the seams, drawing a load, tilt and coals included, of from 12 to 14 cwt.

The Sheltie's lot underground is admittedly a hard one, but his tractable disposition usually ensures for him kindly treatment at the hands of the boy who has him in charge.

These ponies, says Mr. Brydon, were first used in the coal pits of the North of England about the year 1850.

Horse ponies from 3 to 5 years old could then be purchased for £4 10s. each delivered at the collieries.

Since that time prices have risen enormously, though for the smallest animals they fluctuate from time to time in sympathy with the price of coal. As the cause of the influence of the coal market upon the price of Shetland ponies is perhaps not quite obvious, it must be explained that the chief value of these little animals is their ability to work in the low galleries of thin-seamed pits; when the price of coal sinks to a certain point these thin seams cannot be profitably worked, the pits are "laid in," or temporarily closed, and the ponies withdrawn.

In 1891 the average yearling was worth £15 and a two-year-old £18, while full-grown ponies were scarcely procurable. In 1898 a four-year-old could be bought at from £15 to £21, owing to the depression in the price of coals and the suspension of work in thin-seamed pits.

It will be understood that only small animals of the commoner sort suitable for pit work are affected by the coal market. Horse ponies of the right stamp with good pedigree and suitable for the stud still command from £30 to £50, and in some cases even more.

Mare ponies of good pedigree also command high prices; at the last Londonderry sale, the mares, Mr. R. Brydon informs me, sold at an average of £19 per head; but the average obtained for second-class mares would little exceed six guineas per head.

The docility and good temper of the Shetland pony make him, above all, the best and most trustworthy mount for a child. Captain H. Hayes has remarked that "a comparatively high degree of mental (*i.e.*, reasoning) power is not desirable in a horse, because it is apt to make him impatient of control by man."

The Shetland pony is the rule-proving exception; for he combines with the highest order of equine intelligence a disposition curiously free from vice or trickiness. Mr. Brydon has never known a Sheltie withdrawn from a pit as wicked or unmanageable; withdrawal for such reasons being very frequent with ponies of other breeds.

It may be observed that about the middle of the century there were a number of Shelties in Windsor Park, which were used to do various kinds of work.

During recent years a demand for mares for breeding purposes has grown up in America, much to the advantage of the crofter, who finds a market in the colliery districts for horse ponies only.

Many attempts have been made to increase the size of the Sheltie. About the middle of the last century Norwegian pony stallions were introduced into Dunrossness with the result that a distinct variety was established and still continues; this is called the Sumburgh breed; in size these ponies range from 12 hands to 13·2.

Another variety known as the Fetlar breed owes its origin to the introduction by Sir Arthur Nicolson of a Mustang stallion named Bolivar over half a century ago; the Fetlar ponies run from 11 to 13 hands, and are described as remarkably handsome, swift and spirited, but less tractable than the pure Shetlander.

The Sumburgh and Fetlar varieties deserve mention only as experiments; the result having been to increase the height of the pony, it follows, after what has been said on a former page, that these cross-bred animals are of comparatively small value.

Far more importance attaches to the efforts which have been made to improve the pure breed while preserving its diminutive size. The Marquis of Londonderry, some twenty-five years ago, acquired grazings on Bressay and Moss Islands; and having procured the best stock obtainable from all over the Shetlands, began breeding on judicious and methodical lines.

Twelve or fifteen mares with a carefully selected stallion are placed in an enclosure, and the young stock, after weaning, are turned out on the hills; they are hand-fed in winter, but are never given the protection of a roof, whereby their natural hardiness is preserved. The Marquis of Zetland in Unst, and Mr. Bruce in Fair Isle, follow a somewhat similar method of mating and rearing. Messrs.

Anderson & Sons have on Northmavine done much to promote the interests of the breed by purchasing good stallions, often at Lord Londonderry's annual Seaham Harbour Sale, and distributing these over the common pastures.

The benefits which have accrued from this policy are very marked; and though the crofters yield to the temptation of high prices, and sell their best animals for export, the endeavors of the gentlemen named above to maintain the quality of the breed in its native habitat cannot fail to largely counteract the evil results of such sales.

Among the studs on the mainland the best known, perhaps, is that of the Countess of Hopetoun at Linlithgow. Her ladyship's success has been due in no small measure to that beautiful little sire the Monster.

This pony is a perfect example of the Shetland stallion, as may be gathered from his show yard record: he was first in the class for Shetland ponies under 10 hands 2 inches at the Royal Agricultural Society's Show in 1895, at Darlington, and has been preferred by judges to Lord Londonderry's Excellent and the Elsenham pony, Good Friday, Excellent having taken many first prizes, and Good Friday five firsts at the London shows.

Mr. James Bruce has a drove of Shetland ponies at Inverquhomery, Longside, Aberdeenshire. These are descended from two mares and a stallion imported in the year 1889.

Three years ago, Mr. Bruce replenished his breeding stock by the purchase of five more mares. A noteworthy feature of this stud is the color, which in every case is chestnut, Mr. Bruce's 1889 importations being of that rare color among Shelties.

Since the establishment of the *Shetland Pony Stud Book*, several studs have been founded in both Scotland and England. The chief difficulty the owners have to contend with is the proneness towards increase of size due to milder climate and richer feed.

This tendency can only be checked by the periodical importation of stock from the Shetland Isles.

CHILD'S SHETLAND PONY.

The property of Sir WALTER GILBEY, Bart

Engraved by F. Babbage.

H.R.H. THE PRINCESS VICTORIA IN HER PONY PHAETON.

CHAPTER 8

Uses & Characteristics

It would be difficult to name a class of work in which the pony is not employed. He is used by all, from the sovereign to the peasant and costermonger. Pony racing has been recently re-established as a sport after temporary suspension, due to no shortcoming on the pony's side.

It is rare that a meet of hounds is not attended by a sprinkling of ponies carrying future sportsmen and women, and it is safe to assert that every master of hounds and every man who takes his own line across country served his apprenticeship to the saddle on the back of a pony. The reason is that few men who do not learn to ride in early boyhood, when a pony is the only possible mount, completely master the art in later life; hence we meet few good horsemen who do not receive their first riding lessons on a steady pony.

There is no stamp of vehicle which is not drawn by ponies. Her Majesty, for many years, drove a pony in her garden-chair; in double or single harness we find the pony driven in victoria, dog-cart, governess cart, and Irish car; in the tradesman's light van and in the market cart drawing wares of every description; in the itinerant fishmonger's, coster's and hawker's nondescript vehicle.

The country clergyman and doctor would be in sore straits without the thirteen-hand pony, which does a horse's work on one-half a horse's feed and requires no more stable attendance than the gardener or handy man can spare time to give him.

As shown in the foregoing pages, his labors are not confined to saddle and harness; in some parts of the country, he is still used for pack-work, carrying agricultural produce and peats from the hills and moorlands to the farmstead; and in the low seams of the coal-pits which the horse cannot enter he is indispensable.

Large though our native stock of ponies is, we do not breed them in numbers nearly sufficient for our needs, and each year brings thousands of small cheap ponies to our ports from Norway, Sweden and Russia. These, like the gangs purchased from breeders on Exmoor and elsewhere, are driven from one fair to another, to be sold by twos or threes persons who cannot afford to keep a horse but are obliged to provide themselves with a cheap and useful beast for draught or carriage.

It is very generally admitted that the intelligence of the pony is of higher degree than that of the horse; and the fact, we cannot doubt, is attributable to the different conditions under which ponies and horses are reared.

The former, foaled and brought up on the hills and wastes, developed the ability, like other wild animals, to look after themselves, and the intelligence so evolved is transmitted to generations born in domestication. The horse foaled and reared in captivity, with every precaution taken for his security, has no demands made upon his intelligence, and his mental faculties remain to a great extent undeveloped. The same causes operate to furnish the pony's stronger constitution and greater soundness; greater soundness not only in limb but also organic; roaring and whistling are unknown in the pony, common as they are in the horse.

This superiority of constitution accounts for the marked superiority of the pony over the horse in endurance. The small and compact horse is always a better stayer than the large, loosely-built animal, and in the pony we find the merits of compactness at their highest.

Numberless instances of pony endurance might be quoted, but two or three will suffice. Reference has been made to Sir Charles Turner's achievement of riding a pony ten miles and over thirty leaps in forty-seven minutes, and to the conveyance of news from Holyhead to London by relays of ponies at the rate of twenty miles an hour.

Whyte, in his *History of the British Turf*, states that in April, 1754, a mare, 13 hands 3 inches high, belonging to Mr. Daniel Croker, travelled 300 miles on Newmarket Heath in 64 hours 20 minutes; she had been backed to perform the journey in 72 hours, and therefore completed her task with seven hours and forty minutes to spare. Her best day's work was done on Tuesday, April 23. Mr. Whyte gives the following details of this extraordinary performance:

> "24 miles and baited; 24 miles and baited; 24 miles and baited; 36 miles without baiting; total 108 miles. On the Monday and Wednesday, she covered 96 miles each day. She was ridden throughout by a boy who scaled 4 stone 1 lb. without reckoning saddle and bridle. Another performance worth citing as proof of pony endurance was Sir Teddy's race with the London mail coach to Exeter, a distance of 172 miles. Sir Teddy, a twelve-hand pony, was led between two horses all the way, and carried no rider himself. He performed the journey in 23 hours and 20 minutes, beating the coach by fifty-nine minutes."

We generally find that great feats of endurance, involving capacity to thrive on poor and scanty food, have generally been performed by ponies.

In the Nile Campaign of 1885 the 19th Hussars were mounted on Syrian Arabs, averaging 14 hands, which had been purchased in Syria and Lower Egypt at an average price of £18. The weight carried was reduced as much as possible in view of the hard work required of the ponies, but each of the 350 on which the Hussars were mounted carried about 14 stone.

Their march from Korti to Metammeh as part of a flying column showed what these little horses could do; between the 8th and 20th of January, both days included, they travelled 336 miles; halting on the

13th. On the return March from Dongola to Wady Halfa, 250 miles, after nearly nine months' hard work on poor food they averaged 16 miles a day, with one halt of two days.

Colonel Burrow, in reviewing the work performed by these ponies, says:

> "Food was often very limited, and during the desert march, water was very scarce. Under these conditions I venture to think that the performances of the regiment on the Arab ponies will compare with the performance of any horsemen on record."

Captain Fred Burnaby, in his well-known essay "A Ride to Khiva," bears witness to the wonderful endurance of a fourteen-hand Tartar pony which he purchased with misgivings for £5, in default of any better mount.

This pony, he tells us, was in such miserable condition, his men complained among themselves that it would not be worth *eating*, they looked upon the little beast as fore-doomed from the moment Captain Burnaby mounted it.

Yet this pony, its ordinary diet supplemented by a few pounds of barley daily, carried its rider, who weighed twenty stone in his heavy sheepskin clothes, safely and well over 900 miles of bad roads, often through deep snow, and always in bitterly cold weather, the thermometer being frequently many degrees below zero.

On the concluding day of the return journey this pony galloped the last 17 miles in 1 hour and 25 minutes. It would be easy to multiply examples of pony endurance; but we forbear.

The greater stamina of the pony is evidenced in another direction, namely, length of life. Instances in which ponies have attained to a great age are more numerous than those recorded of horses, and further the pony lives longer.

Mr. Edmund F. Dease, of Gaulstown, Co. Westmeath, lost a pony in December, 1894, which had reached the age of 39 years; in 1896,

Mrs. Pratt, of Low Pond House, Bedale, Yorks, lost a pony mare aged 45 years; on Christmas Day, 1863, there died at Silworthy, near Clovelly in North Devon, a pony which had arrived within a few weeks of his sixtieth year.

Accounts of ponies which lived, and in some cases worked, until they reached 40, 38, 37, and 35 years also recur to mind.

There is a degree of cold beyond which the horse cannot exist; and as he approaches the latitude where the limit prevails, the effect of climate is apparent in his conformation.

The frozen and unfriendly country of Lapland has its small ponies; they are employed in drawing sledges over the snow and transporting forage and merchandise, which in summer are conveyed in boats. In Iceland he is dwarfed to a Lilliputian size, and thriving in the comparatively mild climate of the Shetlands we find a pony smaller than any other in the British Islands.

It would seem from the facts it has been possible to collect that the New Forest, Welsh, Exmoor and Dartmoor, Fell and Connemara breeds of ponies are in their natural state of small value to man, though they owe to the natural conditions under which they exist qualities which may be turned to very valuable account by judicious crossing with breeds of a recognized stamp.

Improvement must involve partial sacrifice of qualities such as ability to withstand exposure and cold on insufficient food, sure-footedness, and the sagacity which avoids bog and treacherous ground. These qualities, in their highest development, are indispensable to a wild animal; but the improved pony obtained by crossing is not destined for a wild life on the hills and wastes, and is less dependent upon them.

Partial loss of such attributes, therefore, is a price well worth paying for the increased size and better conformation which render the produce suitable for man's service with the more artificial and luxurious conditions of life inseparable from complete domesticity.

The remarkable soundness of limb and constitution, developed by centuries of free life on the hills, are enduring qualities which appear in generation after generation of stock descended on one side from the half-wild breeds; and these are the qualities which above all it is desirable to breed into our horses of all sizes and for all purposes. The advantage to be gained by systematic improvement of these wild breeds of ponies is therefore not by any means advantageous to one side only.

The Polo Pony Society at their meeting of 7th December, 1898, re-solved to set apart a section of their Stud Book for the registration of Welsh, Exmoor, New Forest and other breeds of ponies; and with ref-erence to this step Lord Arthur Cecil, in his Introduction to the fifth (1899) volume of the Polo Pony Stud Book, says:—

"It is in the limit of height that the greatest difficulty of the So-ciety lies. Could we be certain of breeding every animal between 14 hands and 14 hands 2 inches our course would be tolerably clear.... There is always, however, the danger that the best-looking and best-nourished of our young stock will, if some means be not found to prevent it, exceed this limit.

The remedy is more or less within our reach by utilizing the hardy little stocks of ponies which are to be found almost indige-nous in those districts of the British Isles where there are large tracts of mountain or moorland ground.

I refer to such ponies as those found in North and South Wales, the New Forest, Exmoor, Dartmoor, and the hills of the north of England and west coast of Scotland.... Perhaps it may not be out of place to mention that the present is not an inappro-priate time for upholding the breeding of ponies on hill lands.

The keeping of hill sheep is not so remunerative as of yore, the price of wool being so low and the demand for four-year-old mutton not being anything like what it was a few years ago; whereas, on the other hand, the demand for ponies, especially good ones, is likely to increase, and if farmers will only give them a fair chance they will amply repay them for their keep up to three years old.

It is hoped that by careful consideration of their various characteristics, and by registering such of them as are likely to breed riding ponies, and by periodically going back to this fountain head of all ponies, we may be able to regulate the size of our higher-class riding ponies to the desired limit, while at the same time we shall infuse into their blood the hardiness of constitution and endurance, combined with a fiery yet even temper, so preeminently characteristic of the British native breeds."

The Shetland pony stands upon a different footing. In him we have a pony whose characteristics are equally valuable to it as a wild animal and as one in a state of domestication. It is the only one of our half-wild breeds which gains nothing from an infusion of alien blood; its value depends upon the careful preservation of distinctive peculiarities of size and make, which fit it above all others for special purposes.

THE FIRST LEAP.

From the picture by Sir EDWIN LANDSEER, R.A.

The Shetland Pony today

CHAPTER 9

Breeding Polo Ponies

With only the limited experience in breeding ponies for Polo possessed by all who breed stock, remarks hazarded under this heading must necessarily be guided by general principles of breeding, and readers must be left to take them for what they may be worth.

The steadily increasing popularity of the game of Polo has naturally produced an increased demand for suitable ponies; and Polo players being as a rule wealthy men, to whom a really good animal is cheap at almost any price, the value of first-rate ponies has risen to a level which compels attention to their breeding as a probably remunerative branch of industry.

It was difficult to find ponies when an elastic 14-hand limit was the rule; and if we may judge from the prices which have been paid since the regulation height was raised to 14 hands 2 inches, the greater latitude thus afforded players in selecting mounts has done little or nothing towards solving the difficulty.

What is this Polo Pony for which a fancy price is so readily forthcoming? In the first place, it is not a pony at all, but a small horse; we may let that pass, however. The modern Polo Pony must be big and powerful, at once speedy, sound, handy and docile, having also courage, power to carry weight, and staying power. And, as the necessary speed and courage are rarely to be found apart from blood, it has become an article of faith with players that the first-class pony must have a preponderance of racehorse blood in his veins.

Hence a serious difficulty faces the breeder at the outset. For generations we have devoted all our care to increasing the height of the racehorse, and with such success that in 200 years we have raised his average stature by nearly 2 hands. The great authority Admiral Rous, writing in the year 1860, said that the English racehorse had increased in height an inch in every twenty-five years since the year 1700. We now regard a thoroughbred as under size if he stand less than 15 hands 3 inches.

This is an important point to bear in mind; for if we are to breed blood ponies of 14 hands 2 inches to meet the demand which has recently arisen, it is plain that we must undo most that our fathers and ancestors have done.

A Polo Pony to command a price must be able to carry from 12 to 14 stone and must be sound. Nine stone seven lb. is nowadays considered a crushing burden for a racehorse of 16 hands to carry a mile and a quarter. Never are the weights for a handicap published but the air grows thick with doubts and forebodings as to whether this horse or that can possibly stand the strain required by the handicapper's impost, or whether it is worth risking his valuable legs under such a weight at all. And yet, to a certain extent, it is among small blood horses, no better endowed with bone and no sounder than the big ones, that we seek animals capable of carrying 12 or 14 stone in first-class Polo.

The strain of playing a single "period" in a tournament match, in which the pony is required to make incessant twists, turns, sudden starts at speed, is continually being pulled up short, and is sent short bursts of hard galloping, takes far more out of the pony than does a race out of a racehorse, or an average day's hunting out of the hunter.

The marvel is, not that fast and well-bred ponies capable of doing this should command fancy prices, but that such should be obtainable at any figure.

Under existing conditions, a small blood horse that looks like making a Polo Pony is neither more nor less than an accidental deviation from the normal. It is an accident that his height at five years does not exceed the regulation 14 hands 2 inches; it is an accident—unhappily, a rare one—that he has bone to carry weight; and before the trainer can make a Polo Pony of him he must be fast, handy, kind, and docile—another set of accidents; we might, indeed, almost call the first-rate Polo Pony a phenomenal chapter of accidents.

For let us bear in mind that when we have found our 14 hands 2 inches endowed with the needful make and shape, we have not by any means necessarily got our Polo Pony.

Only the smallest percentage of the thousands of racehorses foaled annually prove good enough to pay their trainers' bills; and when we reflect upon the nature of the work required on the polo ground, the sterling good qualities demanded of a pony for first-class Polo, we should indeed be sanguine did we look for high and uniform merit in the race of animals we hope to found upon a basis of pure blood!

The clean thoroughbred, except in very rare instances, has not the power needful to enable him to stop quickly and turn sharply at the gallop. Speed he has, but he lacks the strong hind-quarters essential to carry 12 or 13 stone.

The pony possessing the needful qualifications of make and shape has yet to be "made;" and only a trainer of experience could tell us what proportion of the likely-looking animals that come into his hands turn out worth the trouble of educating.

Herein we find the reason for the vast difference in value which exists between a pony that is untrained and one which has gone through the various stages of stick-and-ball practice, the bending courses, practice games, and has finally been proven in matches. In the raw state the best-looking 14-hands 2-inch pony is worth £25 to £50; when trained—when he has proved to his exacting trainer's satisfaction that he is a Polo Pony, and does not merely look like one—he is worth, as we know, any sum up to 750 guineas, and there is no reason to suppose that this figure marks the limit which enthusiastic players are prepared to pay; on the contrary, the tendency is to go further.

Such ponies as Mr. George Miller's Jack-in-the-Box, Lord Kensington's Sailor, Captain Renton's Matchbox, Mr. Buckmaster's Bendigo, the late Mr. Dryborough's Mademoiselle, Mr. Walter Jones's Little Fairy, have acquired their fancy value through their amenability to the training which has fitted them for the game.

As to the breeding of these ponies, it is doubtful if their respective owners know as a certainty whether they were got by a thoroughbred pony sire or by an Eastern sire; in the case of many high-class ponies nothing is known of their breeding.

All probably have a strong strain of pure blood in them, but in the absence of certain knowledge concerning their pedigrees they are of comparatively little use to us as object lessons in Polo Pony breeding. Whether, in view of the extremely "accidental" character of the Polo Pony already referred to, that knowledge would be helpful if available is another matter.

And while we make the English Turf pony which can carry weight our ideal, we acknowledge the difficulty of procuring it by seeking ready-made ponies in every corner of the horse-breeding world. Arabs and their near allies—Egyptian, Syrian and Barb ponies; Australian, Argentine, Canadian and Cossack ponies; ponies from the Tarbes district of France; ponies from Texas, Wyoming and Montana—all these have been imported and are played on English Polo grounds, and though not considered equal in speed, bottom, and courage to the English pony, the best of them when "made" are good enough to command high, if not extravagant, prices.

The great object, it is granted once for all, is to get a pony as nearly thoroughbred as possible, for none other is good enough to play in the best class of game. At the same time, a large and representative proportion of players, while heartily granting the superiority of the well-bred pony when it can be obtained, consider it wiser to look the situation squarely in the face and admit that the supply of such ponies cannot be depended on to meet the demand.

If it be a choice between an utterly inadequate supply of English-bred ponies with blood, speed, stamina and weight-carrying power, to be bought only at prices which reserve them to the wealthiest, and a sufficiency of ponies with a strain of alien blood, somewhat less speedy, courageous and enduring, the latter must be chosen; and as already said the Polo Pony Stud Book Society has recognized this by opening sections of their Stud Book for suitable individuals among our Forest and Moorland breeds, with a view of obtaining foundation stock.

We may take it as an axiom in our endeavor to produce a breed of 14-hands 2-inch Polo Ponies that the sire must be a small thoroughbred, or, if not a thoroughbred, an Arab. The reader may be reminded that adoption of this alternative involves no departure from the principle of a pure blood basis.

It was the Arab that laid the foundation of our thoroughbreds in England, and the best horses on the Turf of today may be traced to one of the three famous sires—the Byerly Turk, imported in 1689, the Darley Arabian in 1706, and the Godolphin Arabian in 1730; all of them, it may be remarked, horses under 14 hands 1 inch.

There is, indeed, much to be said in favor of the policy of returning to the original Eastern stock to find suitable sires for our proposed breed of 14-hands 2-inch ponies. While we have been breeding the thoroughbred for speed, and speed only, Arab breeders have continued to breed for stoutness, endurance, and good looks.

By going to Arab stock for our sires we might at the beginning, sacrifice some measure of speed; but what was lost in that respect would be more than compensated by the soundness of constitution and limb which are such conspicuous traits in the Eastern horse.

Furthermore, the difficulty of size, which first of all confronts us in the thoroughbred sire, is much diminished if we adopt the Arab as our foundation sire.

We need not consider the game as played by Orientals. The Manipuris, whose national game it is, and from whom Europeans first learned it, use ponies which do not often exceed 12 hands in height.

As told by Sir Joseph Fayrer in his 1900 classic "*Recollections of my Life*," the game was introduced into India proper in 1864, and first played in England by the officers of the 10th Hussars in the year 1872, upon their return from service in India.

In India, where the game of Polo was first played by Englishmen, the Arab is thought the perfect pony, the more so because the height of ponies played under the Indian Polo Association's code of rules must not exceed 13 hands 3 inches.

The extensive operations of the Civil Veterinary Department have proved again the truth that no sire impresses more certainly and more markedly his likeness upon his stock than the Arab, a fact which is due to the high antiquity, and therefore "fixed" character of the breed.

If, therefore, we find the stock got by the thoroughbred sire too prone to outgrow the limit of height, we may, without self-reproach, turn for assistance to the Eastern stock, from which we have evolved the modern racehorse, as in doing so we shall simply be going a step farther back, and thereby avoid in great measure the difficulty of stature which our fathers and ancestors have created for us in our endeavor to breed a small compact horse from the pure strain.

The next point that presents itself is: on what sort of animal would it be most advisable to cross our thoroughbred or Arab?

In the absence of any long-continued series of experiments, which alone could have led to definite results in the production of a fixed type of pony, or a stamp of pony worth trying to perpetuate as a fixed type, the answer must be conjectural; we can only deal in probabilities.

We may not be able to establish a breed of which a specimen exceeding 14 hands 2 inches shall be something quite abnormal; on the contrary, the whole course of experience in breeding horses of whatever class goes to prove the impossibility of ensuring that the progeny of any given sire and dam shall attain to a specified height, neither less nor more.

Nevertheless, there seems no reason why skill and care in breeding should not in course of time produce an animal whose *average* height at maturity shall be the desired 14 hands 2 inches.

There are, it must be repeated, several essential points to be kept clearly in view in our endeavor to develop a Polo Pony on the foundation of Thoroughbred or Arab blood.

We have primarily to guard against the tendency to exceed the regulation height, and we must seek means to obtain the bone and stamina which are so necessary.

Our Forest and Moorland mares suggest themselves as the material at once suitable for the purpose and easily obtainable. In these ponies we have the small size which will furnish the needful corrective to overgrowth, and we have also that hardiness of constitution and soundness of limb which are invaluable in laying the foundation of our proposed breed of 14-hands 2-inch ponies.

Many attempts have been made from time to time to improve these breeds; indeed, some have been so frequently crossed with outside blood that the purity of the strain has nearly disappeared; this is believed to be the case with the Dartmoor pony.

At the same time these infusions of blood have done nothing to impair the value of the ponies in respect of their intrinsic qualities of hardiness and soundness.

That small thoroughbred and Arab blood blends well with the Forest and Moorland strains has been abundantly proved; Marske, the sire of Eclipse, who was under 14 hands 2 inches, as is well known, stood at service in the New Forest district for three or four seasons from about the year 1765, and produced upon the New Forest breed a beneficial effect which remained in evidence for many years.

The late Prince Consort sent a grey Arab stallion to stand at New Park, which did much good in improving the stamp of pony; and in 1889 as before mentioned Her Majesty lent two Arab sires, which remained respectively for two and three seasons and produced a marked effect on the Forest breed. One of the Dongola Arabs or Barbs which Mr. Knight used gave the best results on the Exmoor ponies, and the use of the thoroughbred horses, Pandarus by Whalebone, and Canopus, grandson of Velocipede, also improved the breed in point of size.

Some of the best hunters in the West of England trace their descent on the dam's side to the Welsh Mountain pony, the sire of some of the best horses, however, being a horse with a stain in his pedigree, viz., Mr. John Hill's Ellesmere by New Oswestry.

In this connection it may be remarked that Bright Pearl, winner in the class for unmade Polo Ponies at the Crystal Palace Pony Show, held in July, 1899, was got by the thoroughbred Pearl Diver out of a Welsh Hill Pony mare whose wonderful jumping powers had gained her many prizes.

The fact that the Forest and Moorland breeds owe their small size to the rigorous conditions of a natural free life and the spare diet accessible must not be lost sight of, for their tendency to increase in size when taken up, sheltered and well fed is very marked.

The fact is of importance, because we could not expect that foals got by a thoroughbred or Arab sire would possess the stamina that enables the Forest or Moorland pony to withstand exposure.

It is true that the stock got by Marske throve under the comparatively mild rigors of New Forest life; but the thoroughbred of 135 years ago was a stouter and hardier animal than is his descendant of to-day. It would therefore be necessary to choose between losing the young half-bred stock altogether, and of rearing it under more or less artificial conditions with the certainty of rearing an animal which would respond to those conditions by increased stature.

The same remarks apply equally to stock got from Forest or Moorland mares by an Arab sire which flourishes in a high temperature but is not adapted to endure continuous cold and damp.

Judgment and care might do something to obviate the tendency to overgrowth; the happy medium to adopt would be to allow the dams with their half-bred youngsters as much liberty as varying climatic conditions indicated the well-being of the latter could withstand.

It has been suggested that the mares which have finished their active career of four or five seasons on the Polo ground might with advantage be used for breeding purposes, being mated with a small Forest or Moorland stallion.

This suggestion does not commend itself to the practical breeder, who is well aware that a big mare throws a big foal even to a small horse. Were increase of size the object in view the worn-out Polo Pony mares might be used thus with every prospect of success; the reverse being our aim, it is to be feared that experiments conducted on these lines would lead to failure.

It is reasonable to think that a breed of small horses can be established by the judicious intermingling of Forest or Moorland mares with Thoroughbred or Arab sires, but past experience in stock-raising has taught breeders that the creation of a new, improved strain, whether of horses, cattle, or other domestic animals, is a slow process.

Failures in breeding must be corrected, and errors retrieved by gradual and cautious steps before we can hope to succeed in creating a breed of ponies true to the required type.

That it can be done with patience and skilled judgment there need be no doubt; but the evolution of the animal required, whether on the thoroughbred foundation or on the original progenitor of the thoroughbred, the Arab, will be a matter of time. It may be that the present generation will lay the foundation of a breed of 14-hands 2-inch Polo Ponies, and that posterity will build the edifice and enjoy the benefits.

To summarize briefly what has been said, the position is this:—

First, ponies with blood, speed, courage, and the many qualities essential to make a first-class Polo Pony are rare. They command fancy prices when trained, but it is only when trained and *proven* that they command high prices.

Second, the difficulty of producing a breed of blood ponies is due to the long-maintained and successful effort to increase the size of the thoroughbred, and the fact that racehorses are bred for speed only, whereas speed is but one of the many qualities essential to the Polo Pony.

Third, and in response to this difficulty, the sire chosen for the foundation stock should be a small and compact Thoroughbred or an Arab. The dam used for foundation stock should be chosen from the best of our Forest or Moorland ponies.

The tendency to undue increase in height should be counteracted in the individual, by a free and natural life as far as climate permits and in the breed, by recourse to further infusion of Forest or Moorland blood when necessary.

ARAB HORSE MESAOUD—14.2 hands.
The property of Mr. WILFRED SCAWEN BLUNT.

From a sketch by H. F. Lucas Lucas.

POLO PONY SAILOR.

The Polo Pony today is sprightly, brave, and athletic.

CHAPTER 10

Ponies Today

In this year 2025, the polo pony occupies a place of singular prestige within the world of equestrian sport. No longer seen merely as the agile workhorse of a gentleman's field game, the modern polo pony is a creature of strategic breeding, rigorous training, and significant investment.

As the sport has grown more global and more competitive, so too has the standard—and the price—of the animals upon which it depends.

Today's top-level polo ponies are the product of decades of refinement, not only in bloodlines but in management and conditioning. Across Argentina, the United Kingdom, the United States, and increasingly in parts of the Middle East and Asia, breeding programs now operate with the precision of elite racing or show jumping stables. The best ponies are bred for acceleration, balance, and responsiveness—qualities that define the rhythm of the modern game, which is faster and more tactical than ever.

The sport's breeding epicenter remains Argentina, where influential bloodlines continue to shape the international market. Stallions such as *Durazno, Machitos Aiken Cura,* and the now-legendary *Open El Padrino* have sired generations of ponies that dominate at the highest levels of competition.

Many of these ponies trace their lineage to Thoroughbred stock, crossed carefully with Criollo mares to produce the ideal balance of stamina, agility, and heart. Argentine breeders, particularly from historic studs like *Los Machitos*, *La Dolfina*, and *Ellerstina*, have become as celebrated in equestrian circles as the players themselves.

Cloning, once a curiosity, is now a quiet but accepted part of the elite game. The clones of *Dolfina Cuartetera*, Adolfo Cambiaso's famed mare, have continued to make headlines on both sides of the Atlantic, with several copies now competing under top players. These ponies possess not only genetic heritage but a sort of brand power—living testaments to the growing fusion of science, sport, and commerce.

At the top tiers of international polo—such as the Argentine Open, the U.S. Open, and the British Gold Cup—ponies are often changed out as frequently as every chukka, with top players rotating through strings of 8 to 12 horses per match. The cost of assembling such a string is no small matter.

In 2025, a well-bred, professionally trained polo pony capable of playing at a 10-goal level can command upwards of $150,000 USD, with some strings valued well into the millions. Many are now owned not by individuals but by syndicates, clubs, or sponsors who view the horse as both an asset and an ambassador.

The elite players themselves—names like *Adolfo Cambiaso Jr.*, *Hilario Ulloa*, *Facundo Pieres*, *Nina Clarkin*, and *Camilo Castagnola*—are not just skilled riders but sophisticated horsemen, deeply involved in their breeding programs. The best among them train daily with their mounts, developing the kind of intuitive, whisper-close communication that turns a good pony into a great one.

Traits most prized include explosive acceleration, balance in the turn, "mouth" or lightness in the bridle, and, above all, heart—the indefinable quality that makes a pony dig deeper as the pressure of the match mounts.

Polo remains, even in its modern form, a sport of elegance and privilege—but it is also one of sweat, skill, and the kind of horsemanship that transcends fashion or fortune.

The 2025 polo pony is a living culmination of centuries of knowledge—rooted in the grasslands of Argentina, refined in breeding barns across the world, and tested in the fierce theatre of the field. As the game evolves, these ponies evolve with it: faster, smarter, and more revered than ever.

Polo ponies move with a kind of urgent poetry—super quick to pivot, instant in their decisions, every stride a negotiation between horse and rider. They carry a different kind of expectation, one measured in bursts and collisions rather than the slow, deliberate sweep of a hunter ring. Yet underneath, the parallels are unmistakable. Balance, elasticity, scope—these are the same traits that define excellence in any ring. A good jumper pony doesn't need to outrun the other horses; it needs to carry its rider over a fence as if the effort were invisible, land, and move on in rhythm, clean and quiet.

There is an artistry in that kind of motion, the same careful economy of movement that polo demands in its own urgent way. Bloodlines whisper through both disciplines, a reminder that athleticism, temperament, and instinct are inherited, honed, and celebrated, whether the field is green with polo goals or fenced in for a hunter course.

Across continents, the world of pony hunters and jumpers occupies a fascinating space between children's sport and high-performance equestrianism.

Globally, the sport forms a kind of informal network, an interlinked constellation of regional traditions, pedigrees, and breeding philosophies that reflect the histories of horses themselves. Bloodlines, both ancient and modern, tell the story of human priorities: the quest for temperament, athleticism, style, and reliability in mounts capable of carrying young riders safely and gracefully. Selective breeding has produced ponies highly specialized athletes, each lineage a living archive of geographical, cultural, and aesthetic imperatives.

Throughout the last century, breeders have tracked movement, conformation, jumping ability, and behavior scientifically, shaping ponies whose capabilities extend beyond their diminutive stature.

In this context, two concepts are central: scope, the pony's athletic potential to jump with power, elasticity, and clean technique, and what it means to be a good mover, a pony whose stride, balance, and rhythm express effortless athleticism whether on the flat or over fences.

In Europe, the United Kingdom remains the historical and spiritual home of pony showing. The hunter pony division evolved from the British field-hunter ideal—a compact, elegant, and mannerly mount capable of carrying young riders across hedges, ditches, and open country. The ancestry of today's show ponies in Welsh, Dartmoor, and Exmoor stock, became more refined through crossings with Arabian, Thoroughbred, and Hackney lines up into the 20th centuries, creating riding ponies: a mount with both refinement and stamina.

The Riding Pony represents a conscious application of equine genetics: careful pairing to combine scope, elegance, and temperament, producing offspring capable of performance and pedagogy simultaneously. A pony's scope reflects its ability to approach, take off, and land over fences with balance, power, and precision, while its status as a good mover signals efficient, ground-covering strides, an uphill, balanced canter, and soft, expressive gaits—qualities that make the pony aesthetically pleasing in the hunter ring and functionally adept in the jumper ring.

Prominent British lines exemplify this history. Bwlch Valentino, a Welsh Section B stallion of the 1970s, combined strength, scope, and an elegant canter that would define the modern hunter movement; his descendants continue to appear in the pedigrees of top small and medium ponies in both Europe and the United States.

Downland Chevalier, a mid-century Riding Pony, exemplified the ideal marriage of refinement and performance, passing on expressive gaits, balanced conformation, and jumping technique that judges still prize today. Cusop Dimension's progeny, with their exceptional movement and calm, responsive temperament, dominate first-ridden and intermediate classes; his influence illustrates how a single stallion can shape traits across multiple generations, particularly elasticity in the trot and carefulness over fences, which directly enhances scope and natural rhythm.

Among modern Welsh Section B lines, the Gayfields Ponies stand out as models of athleticism, temperament, and style. The Gayfields stud has produced a series of high-performing hunters and jumpers whose conformation, scope, and expressive movement exemplify the ideal modern pony, while retaining the spirited yet sweet and manageable temperament that has defined Welsh breeding for centuries.

The Gayfields ponies consistently exhibit balance and carefulness over fences—the hallmarks of scope—and fluid, ground-covering strides and a soft, uphill canter that mark them as good movers. Notable members of the line include a range of ponies celebrated for their rideability, jumping ability, and competition success. Alongside Gayfields, other British studs such as Clovermeade Welsh Ponies, which carry some lines from Gayfields crosses, have produced similarly exceptional mounts. Clovermeade ponies are carefully selected for scope, temperament, and expressive movement, blending refinement with athleticism to create ponies that excel in hunters, jumpers, and equitation. These breeding decisions underscore how legacy traits are propagated across contemporary pony stock.

The National Pony Society (NPS) and British Show Pony Society (BSPS) maintain pedigree documentation, classifying ponies by ancestry and performance. In these systems, judges evaluate execution alongside conformation, turnout, and suitability for a young rider. Leading-line and first-ridden classes are carefully structured pedagogical steps, teaching children the ethics, discipline, and subtlety of equestrian life while celebrating the traits that breeders prefer. Ponies with natural scope can navigate fences with minimal stress, and good movers create the visual elegance and rhythmic consistency that judges prize in the hunter ring.

Ireland has cultivated its own distinct pony identity through the Connemara, a breed that traces back to native Celtic ponies crossed with Arabian stock. Famous bloodlines such as Erne Lady Goldilocks, known for exceptional technique and carefulness, and Hazy Dawn, prized for great temperament and balance, exemplify how centuries of selection have produced ponies suited to a young riders' needs plus rigorous competition.

The Connemara is really a living archive of Irish rural heritage, shaped by environmental pressures and human preference, and its continued exportation demonstrates the influence of historical traits.

Across continental Europe—in France, the Netherlands, and Germany—equestrians have developed sophisticated systems for pony jumping, integrating local breeds with imported British and Irish stock. FEI-sanctioned pony Grand Prix events and the annual European Pony Championships require ponies to navigate courses of technical complexity, demonstrating rhythm, scope, and precise, efficient movement. Breeders there emphasize elasticity, trainability, and carefulness, maintaining studbooks that trace each pony's lineage over ten generations back to ensure predictable conformation, movement, and jumping ability.

Europe provides a blueprint, but the United States has taken that model and reshaped it into a uniquely American ecosystem—larger, and more commercial, but no less exacting. American breeders and trainers import Welsh, British Riding, Connemara, and Dutch ponies, combining them with domestic stock. Breeding strategies often blend the refinement and elasticity of Welsh and Riding Ponies with the power, scope, and rideability of Thoroughbred crosses, producing ponies capable of excelling over fences while remaining manageable for young riders.

Names such as Blueberry Hill, Rollingwoods L On Time, Trillville, and Hi Lite, are more than champions; they are progenitors whose traits—elastic trot, jumping scope, and smooth, rhythmic movement—echo across generations of American ponies. Modern American pony programs have also benefited from work on Gayfields ponies and Clovermeade stock, fostering excellence in U.S. hunter and jumper rings.

The tiered competition structure under the United States Equestrian Federation (USEF), culminating in the USEF Pony Finals at the

Kentucky Horse Park, codifies the athletic and educational dimensions of the sport. Divisions are organized first by discipline—hunter, jumper, and equitation—and then by pony size: small (under 12.2 hands), medium (12.2 to 13.2 hands), and large (13.2 to 14.2 hands). In hunter divisions, judging focuses on rhythm, consistency, form, and the almost theatrical illusion of effortlessness, rewarding good movers whose stride and balance create seamless movement across the ring. The over-fences phase is scored numerically, often out of 100, evaluating both the pony's natural scope and the rider's management. Jumper divisions emphasize accuracy, speed, and adaptability, highlighting ponies with scope to clear technical courses efficiently and safely.

Behind the ponies are the human architects of the sport: trainers, breeders, and parents who make up a multi-generational community. Legendary trainers such as Bill Schaub, Mindy Darst, the late Emil Spadone, and Robin Greenwood have shaped the American pony ring through programs that emphasize correctness, patience, and horsemanship. Many riders who go on to international careers—Jessica Springsteen, Lillie Keenan, Reed Kessler—began their competitive lives on the backs of ponies, learning the delicate geometry of stride, distance, and feel.

Culturally, the pony hunter-jumper world represents a particular kind of American pageantry: immaculate braids, gleaming tack, and the ritualized choreography of horse show mornings. Yet beneath the polish lies a complex pedagogical system. Ponies are teachers, demanding but forgiving, attuned to every shift in balance or confidence. The sport functions as a microcosm of equestrian development, shaping riders' technical abilities, patience, empathy, and resilience.

In recent years, USEF and the U.S. Hunter Jumper Association (USHJA) have expanded opportunities for access and inclusion, creating outreach programs that seek to broaden participation and address the sport's substantial economic barriers. Costs in this arena, have climbed sharply. A proven medium or large pony with top placings at Pony Finals or indoors (such as Washington, Devon, or the National

Horse Show) may fetch between $75,000 and $300,000 USD, and in some cases more. These are not the ponies of village gymkhanas or 4-H pony clubs—though many do begin there—but rather professional athletes, campaigned by junior riders with seasoned coaches, full-time grooms, and rigorous show schedules.

Still, the pony divisions remain aspirational, a mix of heritage, ambition, and artistry that defines much of equestrian culture in the United States.

Globally and domestically, the pony hunter-jumper discipline sits at the intersection of beauty, precision, and growth. From the Welsh hills to Kentucky bluegrass, from FEI Pony Europeans to the luminous ring at Pony Finals, it is a sport built on the paradox of smallness containing greatness—where young riders and their mounts learn, together, how to turn practice into poetry. Lineage—whether Bwlch Valentino, Cusop Dimension, Gayfields Ponies, Clovermeade, or Trillville—forms the genetic backbone; training, patience, and performance bring those genetics to life; and culture—the aesthetics, ritual, and devotion—ensures that the pony remains simultaneously a miniature athlete and a monumental teacher.

Thus, in 2025, whether galloping down a polo field in Palermo or gliding through the hunter ring in Kentucky, the pony holds its ground as one of the most beloved and versatile figures in equestrian sport. Across disciplines, countries, and classes, these small horses continue to carry great dreams—with elegance, power, and no small measure of heart.

Modeling at Pony Finals

Walter Gilbey (1831–1914) was a British wine merchant, author, and passionate breeder of horses, especially known for his contributions to the study and improvement of native pony breeds. His writings, including the influential *Horse Breeding and Management*, reflect a deep understanding of equine history, breeding practices, and the practical uses of ponies in rural and sporting life. Gilbey's work helped to preserve knowledge of Britain's semi-wild ponies and inspired future generations of breeders and equestrians. Beyond his literary contributions, he was also a dedicated advocate for animal welfare and the promotion of responsible breeding.